BUSINESS EXECUTIVES
AND THE HUMANITIES

BUSINESS EXECUTIVES
AND THE HUMANITIES

BY

QUENTIN OLIVER McALLISTER

Meredith College
Raleigh, North Carolina

Bulletin Number Three
The Southern Humanities Conference

THE UNIVERSITY OF NORTH CAROLINA PRESS

1951

To My Wife

PREFACE

THIS BULLETIN reports the results of a nation-wide survey conducted over a period of fifteen months. A full year of planning and preliminary investigation preceded the survey and several months were devoted to the study and organization of materials and to the writing of the report.

I am fortunate to be able to present a broad sampling of executive opinion in many of the major divisions of American business and government. The quality of the letters received is a distinctive feature of the survey. In fact, leading executives, representing all levels of American management in business and in government, have given generously of their valuable time, energy, and thought to the replies to my letter. A list of the executives who placed no restriction upon the use of their names appears in the Appendix. To these and to all the others who helped so much, even though I cannot mention their names, I extend my heartfelt thanks.

All the replies, and the excerpts quoted from them, are to be considered solely as the statement of the opinions, attitudes and viewpoint of the individual who writes the letter and not necessarily as an expression of the policy or practice of his company or department. All the comments, analyses and interpretations which have been included in an attempt to unify the material are mine, and must not be attributed to any person or group contributing information for use in this investigation.

To John Alton McAllister, for his invaluable aid and suggestions throughout the course of this survey, I express my deepest gratitude. I am also most appreciative of the patience and editorial assistance and suggestions of Sturgis E. Leavitt and Thomas B. Stroup. To many persons in the South Atlantic Modern Language Association and in the Southern Humanities Conference, my sincere thanks.

QUENTIN OLIVER MCALLISTER

RALEIGH, NORTH CAROLINA

CONTENTS

BUSINESS EXECUTIVES
AND THE HUMANITIES

I

THE PROJECT
AND THE PROCEDURE

ORIGINALLY the purpose of this study was to investigate vocational opportunities for foreign language students. First sponsored by the Humanities Committee of the South Atlantic Modern Language Association, the work was later taken under the wing of the Southern Humanities Conference and expanded to its present form. Since the broadened scope of the investigation placed modern languages in the logical context of the humanities and of the liberal arts, the change in sponsors was natural and appropriate.

The immediate purpose of the investigation is to find out and to analyze the views of business men, industrialists, and governmental executives concerning the value of liberal arts training in general, and language studies in particular—including English—as a part of a preparation for employment in business, industry, and government. A special effort has been made to learn the nature, location, distribution and extent of the demand for persons prepared in foreign languages.

That American business and American education have complementary interests should be self-evident. American business and industry are consumers of the products of the educational system and are to a large degree dependent on college graduates for the maintenance and development of their activities. American education must consider the needs of the business world in shaping any teaching program. Yet in both groups there are many who are ignorant of, and indifferent to, the attitudes, needs, problems and aspirations of the group with which they are not immediately concerned. Too often business and education, of great potential strength as a team, are divided and weakened by groundless suspicion.

Few, indeed, have been the surveys initiated by academic groups to learn the attitudes, needs, preferences and problems of business and of government. Some surveys have been made, but the field remains largely unexplored. The conclusions drawn in the course of this work must, therefore, rest heavily upon the material compiled. Part of the subject matter favors a statistical presentation, but by far the larger part requires a non-statistical treatment. A numerical report can be made of the number of letters received, the number of favorable replies, and certain other percentages, but such a statistical approach becomes inadequate the moment such things as attitudes, qualities and values are taken under consideration. Furthermore, any attempt to limit the scope of this work entirely to questions and answers to which the statistical method is applicable would have resulted in severe limitation upon the quantity and quality of the replies.

In getting information, the orthodox procedure of sending out mimeographed questionnaires in quantity was rejected. Instead, personal, individual, typed letters were sent out. The statistical purpose was served by the inclusion in every letter of three basic questions around which the whole survey was built. Although the pattern was fitted to each individual case, the basic letter was as follows:

> Dear Sir:
>
> **Under the auspices of the Southern Humanities Conference I am preparing an analysis of the views of business executives and industrialists concerning the value of liberal arts training in general and foreign language studies in particular, especially as part of a preparation for employment in business and industry. It is to be assumed, of course, that such training will be in addition to technical or vocational courses in the curriculum. To narrow the inquiry still further, it is also understood that certain skills must necessarily be learned on the job. Even if your experience leads you to consider technical and scientific skills to be of primary importance, we should be very glad to have your personal comment on the following questions:**
>
> **What relative importance for success in your field do you attach to effective study of such liberal arts subjects as language, including English, and the cultural products of foreign nations?**
>
> **In view of your personal experience, and your knowledge of your firm, what opportunities exist for persons trained in foreign languages?**
>
> **If we assume that personal qualifications are favorable, what special studies, or course combinations, will offer the best**

chances of success in the positions you have in mind?

We would greatly appreciate any comment or suggestion. From letters already received we are led to believe that the forthcoming publication of our material in book form will offer a useful analysis of language, area and cultural studies to personnel officers and executives in many fields, as well as to curriculum makers and others concerned with the proper education of men and women for positions at every level. From another point of view we believe that business will find the material of value as part of an attempt to bring the ideas of business and education closer together and as an effort to formulate a curriculum which will better serve the needs of business and industry.

Any portion of your reply not available for publication should be so designated.

Very truly yours,

Preliminary investigations made by me, surveys already made of vocational opportunities for foreign language students,[1] and common sense, led directly to the tentative conclusion that, although language skills are generally held in high regard by employers, a person trained in foreign languages alone would find little vocational opportunity except in teaching, translating and interpreting. Any other approach to the problem seemed to be quite unrealistic. Hence, the following basic assumption was mentioned in the letter and must be kept in mind throughout this work: a person seeking a position requiring business or technical skill must have minimum competence in that technical field, in addition to competence in foreign languages. Personal qualifications of prospective employees were assumed to be favorable.

In selecting names of those persons to whom the letters were sent special importance was given to the role which the large corporations play in any consideration of employment, and ample attention was given to the selection of representative executives at every level in these firms. The executives, especially those in the upper brackets, answered with gratifying candor and completeness. Indeed, the nature and the quantity of this response is of real significance. Business men *do* care about what goes on in the American classroom. Leaders in business and industry are sincerely interested in the problems of

---

[1] *E.g.*, Huebener, Theodore, "Vocational Opportunities for Foreign Language Students," Third Revised Edition, *Modern Language Journal,* 1949.

education in general, and in English, foreign languages, literature, cultural studies, and the liberal arts in particular.

But the investigation only began with the higher executive group. To obtain a more representative selection, the inquiry was broadened to include executives directly concerned with the selection of employees for the various divisions of companies, both large and small. Letters were directed to personnel managers, office managers, sales managers, planning supervisors, and others in immediate control of employment at every level. Attention was given to the executives of small firms representing various types of business activity.

To this appraisal of the attitudes and opinions of business men has been added a less detailed study of the answers received from governmental executives, usually the chief, or director of the bureau, department, or division under examination.

One thousand letters, essentially like the sample letter quoted, were sent out. Four hundred and thirty-seven answers were received. This high percentage of response is, in itself, significant. Of all the replies received, only twenty-nine were useless for the purpose of providing an answer to at least one of the three basic questions. The four hundred and eight remaining letters, together with the references and published material enclosed with the letters, form the documentation of this report.

Since the word "humanities" plays such a large part in the development of this study, some definition of the term must be attempted. As I understand them, the humanities, or the humane studies, embrace modern and classical languages and literatures, history, philosophy, studies in the philosophy of religion and in Biblical literature, art, music, and psychology and the social sciences, insofar as these last disciplines come under the general heading of philosophy, rather than under that of science.

I have approached the writing of this report in the atmosphere of the following conception of the nature of the "humanities." The word is used here to refer to those elements in formal, liberal education which contribute most to the mental cultivation and to the enrichment of the personality and philosophical outlook of the individual. Mental cultivation is taken to mean the development of clear, logical habits and patterns of thinking, a devotion to truth, and an acceptable standard of good taste. Moral and aesthetic consideration of that which is good and that which is beautiful is assumed to be a part of this mental cultivation. Such a development of the mind assumes also the acquisition of necessary, important factual knowledge, and training in the control and use of this knowledge.

Although training and factual knowledge must be broad enough to permit the greatest possible degree of flexibility, a proper discipline in the choice of educational materials and contacts must be maintained. The enrichment of the personality and of the philosophical outlook takes for granted an educational program which requires the individual to rise to meet the challenge of the greatest thought and of the highest artistic achievements of great men and superior minds. Broad contact and frequent association with the greatest and best that man has produced add new facets to the personality of the individual in such a way as to permit him to adjust more successfully and more easily to any situation at any level of human endeavor. This is one of the basic claims for the humanities and for a liberal education in general. In brief, the humanities are regarded by some as the educational means through which the individual may be brought to his fullest and highest development as a dignified, responsible, creative member of society.

Some prominent academic leaders take for granted that there is intrinsic merit in studying languages and culture just for their own sake and that the humanities are the sciences which help us to get into other peoples' minds. As such, the humane studies are called "the useful studies," since "the understanding of the world around us is weakest at this point." However, claims of this nature do not seem to represent an argument which will convince many beyond the circle of those who know from experience what the humanities have to offer.

On the other hand, if this survey brings forth significant support for the contention that the humanities have a practical value, not the least result will be that of throwing into question the direction and emphasis of important segments of the American educational system. Indeed, the very basis of many popular conceptions of the purpose of an education may be challenged.

II

THE VALUE OF ENGLISH IN
BUSINESS AND INDUSTRY

THE BASIC LETTER sent to the business men whose answers provide the material for this study contained only two words of specific reference to English: "including English." Yet the replies plainly indicated that English holds top rank among all the subjects listed under the humanities.

Out of a total of 156 letters of reply stressing the value of English study, seventy-five contained material worthy of special attention. However, only a sampling of typical letters can be offered here.

Many of the statements concerning English stress the practical nature of English. The broad claim of Tracy Higgins, President of the Higgins Ink Company, Inc., offers a good beginning: "English is of primary value, for unless a man can write and speak effectively, he is lost." B. B. Bowen, Assistant Vice President of the Union Planters National Bank and Trust Company, Memphis, Tennessee, is in full agreement with Mr. Higgins, since he finds "a thorough knowledge of English essential to every job, no matter what type." Emilio Desvernine, Jr., of the Publicity Department, Socony-Vacuum Oil Company, makes even more precise the applications of a good knowledge of English: "With the few exceptions of those jobs involving manual labor, the company takes for granted that the applicant must have a good knowledge of English." Whether or not applicants who have the necessary knowledge of English are easily available may best be judged after consideration of the critical statements on English preparation given near the end of this chapter.

J. W. Hathaway, Employment Manager for Sharp and Dohme, Inc., comments on the importance of English in certain cases: "Naturally, English is of tremendous importance in all levels and the test which we use for supervisory selection is almost entirely a test of verbal ability." Many other letters also make it apparent that a definite relation exists between verbal ability and possibility of advancement to higher positions.

Almost without exception, where English is mentioned in the replies it is considered a primary element in every educational program. R. L. Collier, Executive Vice President of the Gray Iron Founders' Society, Inc., feels that an excellent knowledge of English is necessary because it will fit the student for his subsequent business life. This thorough knowledge, according to Mr. Collier, "will provide him with a means of expression without which any amount of excellence he may possess, in either the technical or commercial field, cannot be successfully made known to those who will appraise his work. . . ."

Several recent surveys of business and educational groups have also indicated that English is a subject of the very first importance in any preparation for positions in management, but these surveys stressed primarily the oral and written skills. The present study extends this emphasis beyond the immediate aims of the functional skills to include general abilities and ultimate aims, such as the training of the student to think clearly, logically and effectively, and the enrichment of his cultural experience. In this connection the study of English literature is presented as having real, practical value, especially as part of the general education of those who aspire to executive positions in the business world.

The most notable characteristic of the replies to my letter was the manner in which the business men took for granted that language study, English and foreign, would improve the general mental powers, such as the ability to use the mind in orderly, effective fashion. This point was repeatedly brought out in comments on the role of language in the communication of ideas.

J. H. Holmes, answering for Harold H. Swift, President of Swift and Company, recognizes the importance of "languages, especially English," to the transmission of ideas, either orally or in writing. W. P. Marshall, President of the Western Union Telegraph Company, emphasizes further the key importance of the art of communication: "Certainly I should put very high among the liberal arts the study of English. No matter what an individual's field of occupation may be, there is scarcely any pursuit in which the art of communication is not of the highest importance. I believe that this has been increasingly true in recent years, as human relations have been brought to the fore and generally recognized as a major consideration in enlightened management labor relations."

Mr. Marshall brought out in this quotation a relationship which found repeated expression in the replies, both directly and by implication. The relationship is that of language study to the communication of ideas and, in turn, of communication of ideas to human relations, with particular reference to better understanding between groups. Since detailed consideration of this conception does not fall within the scope of this report, only passing reference to the appearance of the idea in high executive places is possible, but this concept seems to be assuming considerable importance in some divisions of management.

Present in many letters is the thought that adequate communication brings a better chance of understanding. But the transmission of ideas must also be convincing. The need for the ability to speak and write persuasively is closely related to the problem of better human relations. Persons who possess such persuasive abilities in high degree are much in demand by groups which have become painfully aware that they have failed completely to explain to other groups their attitudes, aspirations, and achievements. Business offers a number of positions to persons capable of transmitting ideas convincingly. But advertising firms, as specialists in the field, are more keenly aware than others, perhaps, of the importance of such abilities. Virgil D. Reed, Assistant Director of Research, J. Walter Thompson Company, reports: "There is no question in my mind as to the necessity for a sound training in languages with particular stress on a good command of English and the ability to use it convincingly. Success in our field is dependent entirely upon the ability to communicate ideas convincingly."

Business men who are in daily contact with the public have become sharply aware of the need for men who can speak well. J. Barclay Potts, Vice President, Manhattan Storage and Warehouse, reports: "It is obvious that a command of the English language is important in a business where there is daily contact with the public and this is very important when there is nothing to sell except service."

Daily and direct contact with the public is particularly frequent in the field of merchandising in general, and in department store work in particular. John J. McCarthy, Assistant General Manager, Gimbel Brothers, New York, speaks from experience in his field: "It is my considered opinion that above all other subjects, English is of paramount importance. The number of people that fail to survive the ordeal of an employment interview because of their lack of common English is amazing. Time after time, it is possible to see people with responsible positions fail to secure their immediate and long range goals because of (a) their failure to make themselves understood and

(b) the poor impression they make in speaking." This statement is an example of a constantly recurring theme: business must have persons with more and better preparation in the oral use of language. This is not to say that other skills, both specific and general, are less needed.

The failure of men to advance in their profession because of inadequate English, oral or written, is evidently quite common, if one is to judge from the number of letters like one by W. L. Johnson, Director of Personnel and Industrial Relations, Bell and Howell Company: "On some occasions in the past several years instances have come to our attention where possible promotions have been reconsidered because of the individual's inability to effectively speak and write English. This failing has not only been evident in some of our established personnel but also in new applicants—including college graduates. Certainly we feel that effective speech and writing is a necessary requisite for our executive level personnel and perhaps too little attention has been given this requisite. In our opinion it would be well for college students to consider effective speech and writing of great importance and study programs should be planned to include enough English to permit some measure of accomplishment."

Ambitious persons who seek only the further development of their business specialty or technical specialty as a means of obtaining advancement may find that such an approach will not assure the desired results. Students and those already in business and industrial fields may find that they would have been better off to take additional work in English and the humanities instead of extra courses in accounting or engineering. If the information received is any indication, adult classes, night classes, and private study programs would gain by a shift of emphasis to the essential foundation of general studies, especially language—with particular attention to English.

These last comments are equally applicable to those who seek employment and advancement in governmental service. W. W. Butterworth, while Director for Far Eastern Affairs, Department of State, wrote that: "It is essential that an officer doing political work in one of the geographic offices of the Department should be well grounded in the English language. All too often it has been my experience that an exceedingly promising officer lacked the ability to draft, which has precluded his advancement into the most responsible positions." The importance of ability to draft reports and official documents is mentioned in a publication of the Department of State. The section reads, in part: "Skill at written composition is required for the difficult tasks of draftsmanship which are inseparable from the work of the diplomatic profession. In addition, the Foreign Service officer must be highly trained in oral English; the individual whose speech is halting, awkward or incorrect could not function effectively as an officer."[1]

Many other statements from officials in the Department of State and in other departments of governmental service, show the same attitude toward the importance of English.

When Mr. Butterworth used the words "advancement into the most responsible positions," he touched upon the important matter of leadership and executive capacity. The information compiled is decisively in favor of relating the effective use of English closely and directly to managerial skills. In this connection, Frederick G. Atkinson, Director of Personnel and Industrial Relations, R. H. Macy Company, Inc., calls the ability to express oneself indispensable: "The study of languages, particularly English, improves the individual's ability to express himself, a skill which is indispensable to managerial responsibility." George Wilgus, Personnel Director of the Mutual Life Insurance Company, reports that 1700 persons work in the Home Office of his company. His experience with these and other groups leads him to say that a liberal arts course which includes English is very important to one who expects to attain and hold a position of responsibility. He continues: "It is quite important for supervisors, staff people and junior officers to be able to express themselves simply, clearly and well in memoranda and reports which they must write for their superiors. All too often there is a lack on the part of college trained personnel of facility in using the English language." There is more to be said about the deficiency just mentioned. But first, some notice must be taken of the many letters which presented in detail what the writers believed should be included in any good preparation in English.

Houlder Hudgins, President of the Sloane-Blabon Corporation, says: "In the selection of new employees, we give considerable weight to the effective use of language. Extensive vocabulary, and the ability to use it, ranks high in the list of necesary tools for a successful career in this business." R. L. White, Treasurer, Tennessee Eastman Corporation, finds that training in English aids materially in readily understanding ideas of others and in presenting one's own ideas on any subject. Vocabulary is a major concern in such training. As Mr. White puts it, "A large vocabulary and the ability to use that vocabulary are im-

[1] *The Foreign Service of the United States.* Department of State, Publication 2991, 1948, p. 4.

portant in presenting ideas and thereby attaining respect for one's opinions."

In the acquisition of a large vocabulary and in the development of other faculties, the study of English literature assumes importance in any educational program designed to prepare a student for employment in business. Like many other business men, Henry W. Francis, Vice President of the Francis Metal Products Company, finds a grounding in English literature and a good course in Business English a minimum language study requirement for commercial purposes. Walter S. Tower, President, American Iron and Steel Institute, writes that first and foremost among liberal arts subjects he would include the study of English, both as literature and in composition. He goes on to say: "I doubt whether there is any greater continuing asset than the ability to use English effectively. Certainly there is no greater enjoyment than what is to be found in English literature."

John N. McDonnell, Vice President, The Schering Corporation, summarizes very well the pattern of the replies on the subject of English literature: "A mastery of English literature, while not absolutely essential, is to be considered as almost a nucleus or foundation for a liberal education. Although seldom used as such in business, a knowledge of the good literature in English and as translated prepares the mind of the college student to grasp the thinking of the day. The wisdom of the outstanding writers of the past certainly provides the full value of experience to an individual equal to that which only could be gained by him through several decades of hard, practical contact with the world." This last statement deserves careful consideration by those who feel that the whole job can be done by experience alone.

Henry W. Francis, whose statement was introduced above, strikes a note in his letter which offers a point of departure for a discussion of the importance of English as a part of technical and engineering education. He feels that the high standards of precision demanded, for example, in architectural design should be equalled by the exactitude and quality of the English used in the statement of specifications affecting such design and in verbal or written description of it. In order to acquire such precision, the technical student must give adequate place to language, for, as Mr. Francis says: "Precision of thought, as well as of expression, is dependent upon precision in language, which is the tool of thought."

L. T. Hallet, Chairman, College Recruiting Committee, General Aniline and Film Corporation, in speaking of the training of college personnel hired for technical posts, emphasizes both the oral and written skills. Mr. Hallet finds that effective training in English for such personnel is urgently needed, particularly in view of the fact that so many college graduates fail to meet the minimum standards of his company. R. L. Mason, Manager, Employee Relations Department, Standard Oil Company of New Jersey, agrees with Mr. Hallet on the importance of English, and lays special emphasis upon English composition, report and letter writing. In fact, the Standard Oil Company of New Jersey considers this work so important that it is providing specialized training of this type for its employees, including executive personnel, at its own expense and on company time.

Kenneth A. Meade, Director of College and University Relations, General Motors Corporation, says that his company recruits college graduates largely in the fields of engineering and business administration. In both cases, the company is particularly interested in individuals who can express themselves well, both orally and in written reports. The importance of English in technical executive positions is brought out by Harris Reinhardt, Employment and Training Division, Industrial Relations Department, Sylvania Electric Products Corporation, answering for the president of the firm: "We consider a good working knowledge of the English language an essential part of the technical training which every college graduate must have to get beyond a purely technical position in our organization." General Brehon Somervell (Retired, U. S. Army), now President of the Koppers Company, Inc., is positive in his statement: "There is no question but that a further study of English would be helpful to all engineers." Philip D. Reed, Chairman of the Board of the General Electric Corporation, stresses the value of the fundamentals of English: "The fundamentals of English, if properly taught, are of great value because all our people, whether they be scientific, technical, accounting, sales, etc., are on occasion required to make speeches and write articles which convey thoughts to others. Ability to express oneself clearly is therefore an asset to anyone who aspires to high position in industry." Mr. Reed has offered here specific reasons why persons in all the fields mentioned need to be able to speak and write well. Although he notes the importance of English to those who aspire to high position, it is clear from his statement that these same skills are real assets to anyone who seeks employment with firms like his.

Mr. Reed's words "if properly taught" imply failure on the part of someone to teach the fundamentals of English. Many of the letters of reply were more direct in their criticism. Indeed, concern about the lack of adequate training in English was expressed so frequently that special attention must be paid to these critical statements. The authors of some of the more severely critical letters refused permission to quote, but others were frank and open in expressing their feeling of dissatisfaction.

Clarence I. Blau, Acting Director, Areas Division, Department of Commerce, Office of International Trade, offers the following: "Even more important than foreign languages is an ability to use the English language orally and in writing both concisely and precisely. We find that very few college students can." Wesley Greene, President, International Film Bureau, Inc., makes this statement: "I imagine most businesses are searching for employees who can read and write the English language. We find that practically all high school graduates do not have vocabularies sufficient to cope with the language used by the officers of larger corporations."

A similar criticism is made of college preparation by D. R. Munsick, Sales Manager, the Interchemical Corporation. Following a statement on foreign languages, he says: ". . . a knowledge of the English language, so woefully neglected in our schools and colleges at the present time, is of far greater importance in our particular field of endeavor." R. Vizcarrondo, Foreign Sales Manager, Baldwin Piano Company, is even more specific: "In my estimation, American schools and colleges do not give the subject of English sufficient importance, judging from the lack of good spelling, punctuation and proper grammar used even by college graduates whom I have hired for export work." Roger Albright, Educational Director, Motion Picture Association of America, finds that: "There isn't enough difference between those who have had the advantages of a college education and those who have not in the ability to use the right word at the right place, and in the ability to give oral expression to one's ideas with simplicity and effectiveness."

John N. McDonnell, Vice President, Schering Corporation, has this to say about scientific and technical specialists: "Too few specialists in the technical and scientific fields, such as the chemists, pharmacists, engineers, and others, are skilled in simple composition, grammar, and spelling. This is not a criticism of college training, of course, but instead rests as an indictment of secondary school education." The effect of insufficient training in English apparently is felt at all levels in the business world.

Where is the blame placed by those who make these critical remarks about the products of our classrooms? A few business men call it a reflection on our educational system. Others insist that the fault does not lie with the college teacher, but with the poor work being done in the secondary schools. Still others are not concerned with placing the blame; they simply plead for graduates of our schools and colleges who can read and write in an adequate manner.

Since the teachers are keenly aware of the situation, they are doing all they can to make their work more effective. A discussion of the obstacles faced by the teachers in this matter lies beyond the scope of this report. Yet it may be helpful to show how similar are the wants and preferences of both business men and English teachers in the matter of training in English. The following lines taken directly from letters used in this investigation could just as well have come from teachers of English. Business, for example, seeks in the college graduate the ability "to express himself clearly, logically, and effectively," . . . "to speak and write concisely," . . . "to brief and draft concise, persuasive reports," . . . "to use good English, orally and in writing," . . . "to be not only articulate, but forcefully so," . . . "to know the root sources and origins of words," . . . "to avoid artificial or affected English," . . . "to transmit thought in colorful, easily understood language," . . . "to be able to use the dictionary and to punctuate properly," . . . "to communicate ideas convincingly," . . . "to use correct spelling and grammar," . . . "to use effective, clear, concise, short words and sentences," . . . "to avoid colloquial expressions, puns, and sectional phrases," . . . "to understand readily the spoken and written language of others," . . . "to express oneself accurately on paper, producing satisfactory and finished reports, memoranda and briefs which do not require a lot of editing and revision before they can be approved," . . . "to acquire and use effectively a large vocabulary."

There are also strong recommendations for more oral and written practice, for some attention to Business English and the preparation of briefs, memoranda and reports, for a thorough grounding in English literature, and for more time to be allotted to the study of the English language and literature, particularly for technical students. Indeed, business men and teachers of English are in surprising agreement on the questions of objectives.

As a matter of fact, except for some added emphasis upon vocabulary and written forms common to business, the views of business men are in essential accord with the traditional aims of English teaching programs. The word "traditional" is used intentionally, since business men would include as an important part of class work full consideration of grammar and syntax. Furthermore, some say that through analysis and interpretation of form and content the student may be helped to form clear, orderly thinking habits. It does not seem that the functional approach, so much in vogue today, which neglects such things, is acceptable in principle or effective in practice. There is even some support for the study of the historical development of English, presumably at the higher levels of college work. This attitude is of particular interest in view of some recent attempts to exclude such study from undergraduate programs on the ground that it is appropriate for specialists only.

Many replies urged that more time be given the study of English in the schools. More time is needed, but it does not seem—in the light of my information—that additional time, without a return to fundamentals, would solve the problem. The following statement by Helen M. Harding, an undergraduate English major and a Latin minor who entered business and later became export manager of the Doall Company, touches directly upon the need of fundamental knowledge as a background for emphasis on the functional skills: "I consider it impossible to overestimate the study of English as the foundation for any kind of future work, not minimizing business and industry. It is useless for stenographers to be drilled to take upwards of 140 words a minute when they have no idea of the meaning of the words, and thus can hardly use a dictionary intelligently—to say nothing of punctuation! It is equally futile for one to study the tricks and skills of ad writing or attempt to be an effective journalist without a thorough grounding in our native language and its usage; it follows too logically that a professional man or executive is limited at once in his work if without the proper background in English he is unable to express himself clearly and effectively."

Here is a clear indictment of the all too prevalent tendency to consider only surface techniques. The full weight of opinion expressed in the materials of this survey stands against any neglect of spelling, grammar, syntax, and fundamental skills in reading *with understanding,* writing and speaking. There is a strong stand for the reading of good literature as an essential part of any preparation for positions in business, industry and government, however technical these positions may be.

Plainly, teachers of the English language and literature have reason to take heart. The importance of their role is widely recognized. The teachers and those who have criticized the performance of their products are ultimately in agreement. They agree on the practical importance of the teacher's role, on immediate and ultimate objectives, and the need for doing a better job. The opportunity plainly exists for a new and more intelligent cooperation between business and education, and for a consequent strengthening of our educational system.

So many business men reported the beneficial effect of study of foreign languages upon the ability to use English that some attention must be given to these views. Without thinking of the transfer of learning as a scientific problem, these business men take its existence for granted. They consider the study of foreign languages as having specific, beneficial effect upon such skills as reading, writing, speaking and understanding English. A few quotations will illustrate.

R. Vizcarrondo, of the Baldwin Piano Company, expresses this view briefly and concisely: "I have noticed that those trained in foreign languages are better English scholars than those who have not been so trained. This proves that the study of foreign languages also improves one's English grammar and vocabulary." Philip B. Deane, Foreign Division, Read Machinery Division, Standard Stoker Company, says: "No doubt you have found that your students have improved their English in conjunction with the study of other languages. Translation into or from a foreign language generally clarifies our own tongue and tends to eliminate slang expressions, which are almost impossible for a foreigner to translate and extremely difficult to translate in writing." Roger R. Dulong, Carter Carburetor Corporation, writes: "Primarily, we consider foreign languages as an excellent background for English, vocabulary building and understanding."

Thomas I. Parkinson, President of the Equitable Life Assurance Society, suggests that the primary importance of foreign languages to his firm lies in the improvement which their study brings to English: "Many students of foreign languages are proficient in English and with this qualification can render valuable service in our work. Verbal and written communication with four million members of the Society is an illustration."

Kendall A. Redfield, President, Asgrow Export Corporation, feels that an electrical engineer "simply *must* have the ability to express himself clearly, both to ask questions, indicate that he understands the subject, and in giving instructions to others. If the man has a good grasp of English and a good vocabulary, these will come much easier. If he does have a command of English, it will improve as he studies a foreign language because it will excite his natural curiosity as to the origins of words, differences or similarities of idiomatic expressions, etc." R. L. Collier, Vice President, Gray Iron Founders' Society, adds the following to a statement about the study of foreign languages: "It will, of course, give him the mental gymnastics necessary in understanding and perhaps speaking and writing the language, and in case of several languages, it will help provide him with the root sources which will help him to break down any English term which stems from such roots." Elmer Krueger, President, Paper Art Company, Inc., believes in the greater contribution of more than one foreign language to the improvement of a student's English: "We feel that a good business executive should be well trained in the English language particularly. If it takes one or two foreign languages to accomplish this, as I believe it does, that should be part of the study."

Closely allied to the question of benefits to be had through transfer from modern languages is that of the similar contribution to be had through study of the ancient languages. More than a little support is to be found for the inclusion of Latin, at least in the high school curriculum. In fact, many of our present language ills are blamed on "dismissing Latin so easily in the high schools." A good example of statements about the value of Latin appears in the letter from Emil Schram, President of the New York Stock Exchange: "The study of language is basically important in all fields as it enlarges the student's ability to observe the significant. It seems to me that this is particularly true of Latin. Although it is hard to particularize, Latin gives a student a basic understanding of all the modern languages, and the reading of the speeches of the Roman orators, particularly Cicero, enables him to use logic more effectively as a means of persuasion."

Charles S. Campbell, President of J. B. Williams Company, says: "I belong to that old school group which believes that one benefits by the study of Latin or Greek, or both." Roger Albright, Director, Educational Services, Motion Pictures Producers Association of America, Inc., offers his personal viewpoint: "I happen to believe very strongly in having students well acquainted with Latin and Greek structures and vocabulary, and in some familiarity with the modern languages." Robert E. Wilson, Chairman of the Board, Standard Oil Company (Indiana), puts the ancient and modern languages together in speaking of the contribution of the study of foreign languages to English: "A knowledge of Latin and German certainly helps a man with his English."

Such recognition of contributions of the study of ancient and modern languages in the acquisition of a better knowledge of English points up the important role of English in any preparation for business, industry or government. Many leaders in these fields have been quick to observe and criticize divisions of the American educational system which fail to give English the place and the emphasis which it needs and deserves. Indeed, anything less than first place in the curriculum is not enough. That practical men in commercial and technical pursuits rate such language study higher than any kind of vocational training is significant. Even more, it is a recognition of the need for strengthening college and high school curricula so as to assure general competence in the most basic of all subjects, our own language.

III

THE IMPORTANCE OF THE STUDY
OF FOREIGN LANGUAGES

PROFESSIONAL EDUCATORS, bent apparently upon their own preconceived theories and oblivious of the facts of life as the work-a-day world sees them, find little practical value in the study of foreign languages. Furthermore, they would have students, parents and college administrators believe that foreign language study does not offer job and salary-getting possibilities equivalent to those of technical, commercial and technique-stressing courses. The error inherent in such a concept can be revealed only by obtaining the opinion of those persons most likely to be aware of actual prerequisites for employment, that is, successful American business men. Only they can assess the practical value of language study. Accordingly, it is the purpose of this chapter to show to what extent employers in a wide variety of fields accept foreign languages as practical studies leading to gainful employment and increased opportunity.

What do American business and governmental executives think of foreign languages as part of a preparation for a business career? What are the possibilities for employment of a person adequately trained in foreign language skills who offers in addition commercial or technical abilities?

As was pointed out in the opening chapter, work already done in the field and my own preliminary investigations led to the conclusion that language study, in and of itself, does not open up a large field of opportunity for employment. The persons who answered the following question were asked to assume that language skills would be accompanied by a minimum of competence in technical or commercial skills. Here, then, is the central question in my letter of inquiry:

> What relative importance for success in your field do you attach to effective study of such liberal arts subjects as language, including English, and the cultural products of foreign nations?

Before offering my count of the answers to this question, a word must be said about method, and terms. Letters rated as "Favorable" include a direct statement of a favorable personal attitude of the executive, or of the employment policy of the company, or of opportunities for employment which require a knowledge of foreign languages. Letters which stated that the writer did not know of any jobs in his firm which required a knowledge of foreign languages were called "Unfavorable." Letters called "Neutral" included no direct answer to the question and listed no positions which require a knowledge of foreign languages. Replies listed under this heading cannot be called unfavorable, since sixty-five of them show a high regard for foreign language study, although they did not answer the question concerning the relation between such study and jobs in business and industry.

A count of the answers to my question yielded the following results:

Number of letters sent out.................1000
Number of answers received.............. 437
Favorable................................. 313
Unfavorable.............................. 30
Neutral.................................. 94

This is to say that 91% of the total number of usable letters (343, or the number of answers received minus the number of letters called "Neutral") were favorable. From another point of view, 72% of the *total number of letters received,* without omitting even the "Mr. Jones is out of town" replies, were favorable. From either point of view, here is strong support for the inclusion of foreign language study in *any* preparation for positions in business and in government. Beyond any doubt, if these results are representative of the field—and there is every reason to believe that they are—the experienced executives in business and government support the thesis that foreign languages are desirable, even essential, to the preparation of those who will find employment with American business firms and the Federal government.

Stanley E. Hollis, President, American Foreign Credit Underwriters Corporation, a world-wide trade and credit service, which publishes *Exporters' Digest, America Industrial,* and *Market Guide for Latin America,* is certainly in a position to judge the number of vocational opportunities existing for persons who offer foreign language in combination with knowledge of business principles and practice. The information which he has packed into his letter deserves quotation in some detail:

"As an organization serving American exporters, we can say that a very great number of vocational opportunities have come to our attention for men and women who combine facility in foreign languages with knowledge of business principles and practice, especially merchandising knowledge.

"Export sales departments of manufacturing and merchant firms throughout the country are constantly in search of men and women who read, write and speak Spanish, Portuguese, French, etc., to handle correspondence, advertising and publicity material, to deal with visitors from abroad and, at times, to go out into the foreign field and do sales, market research, advertising and other types of work.

"Manufacturers of industrial equipment, engineering organizations and the like of course prefer those who combine foreign language skill with engineering training. Other specialized fields naturally have their own requirements.

"There can be no doubt that Americans who add modern language skills to their other training definitely enhance their value to any employer."

W. H. Stanley, Vice President of the William Wrigley Jr. Company, expresses this view: "Modern languages are becoming more and more a part of our daily life, and the vista of one who could read foreign languages is immeasurably widened by that fact. . . . Unfortunately, there is a great dearth of people in this country with knowledge of commercial language and sufficient training to occupy the medium and upper positions in large firms, and resort is often taken to employing foreigners for such duties."

The statement of E. W. Amardeil, Manager, Whitney National Bank, New Orleans, supports the view that there is practical use for an adequate knowledge of foreign languages, but that such knowledge should be coupled with the study of subjects relating to the line of endeavor the candidate proposes to enter. Mr. Amardeil goes on to say, ". . . the advisability of learning a foreign language can be taken for granted, if the studies in this field are pursued to the point where the individual does not have a mere working knowledge, but becomes thoroughly conversant with it." Mr. Amardeil feels that there is little doubt that this accomplishment can be put to practical use.

The importance of language study for use in commerce is seen in the remarks by Viola A. Asselin, Export-Import Manager, Brown and Bigelow Company: "The opportunities for American students with language qualifications, I would say, are very great. However, practical grasp of the language is necessary. Language skills are held in very high regard and are a basic requirement for real growth in this field." Charles S. Campbell, President of the J. B. Williams Company, says: "I am a great believer in the value of liberal arts training in general and of foreign language studies in particular." Samuel S. Ericsson, of the Chamber of Commerce of the United States, sees foreign languages as having importance for the business man in general: "For the American business man in general, foreign language training has importance as a secondary qualification insofar as it increases the general scope of understanding and appreciation of the world's problems. In the field of foreign commerce, foreign language training may be of great specific value, but its primary value remains not so much in the ability to read the language as to understand the background and thinking of those whose language is foreign to ours."

The contribution of foreign language study to understanding the thoughts of others is also brought out by H. G. Evans, Vice President of the Hamilton Manufacturing Company, Two Rivers, Wisconsin: "The prime purpose of a study of a foreign language from our viewpoint, in the light of our requirements, would be to enrich and enlarge the use of the English language, thought and wordwise. . . . To think in another language, to better express one's thoughts and understand the thoughts of others, will enlarge one's horizon mentally." At least 25% of the letters received show a serious concern about the lack of "enlarged mental horizons" today. Writers who took note of this lack of the broad view see an increased emphasis upon foreign languages and the humanities in general as an important factor in any attempt to improve human relations.

W. C. Fay, Personnel Manager, American Optical Company, points out the value of language study as an aid in obtaining employment: "Opportunities certainly exist for foreign language students, particularly in the large metropolitan areas such as New York and Boston. It is our understanding that there are more jobs available for such students than there are students for such jobs. It is further our understanding, and our experience, that knowledge of two languages— Spanish being one of these—will help the graduating student to obtain employment more quickly. . . . One thing in which you might be interested is the fact that in our own business we conduct language refresher and strengthener courses through the assistance of professional instructors." The practice of offering language courses to employees on company time and at company expense is quite common. A number of firms reported such courses as necessary and useful.

Languages offer an opportunity for profit and pleasure, in the opinion of Henry W. Francis, Vice President, Francis Metal Products Company: "The command of a second language opens reservoirs of stored thought and experience not otherwise directly available, broadens the perceptions and enlarges the opportunities for profit and pleasure." It would be difficult to find a more succinct statement of the values and purposes of foreign language study than the one just quoted. Obviously, professors of the humanities are not the only ones who see language study in this light. Many business executives express their faith in both the profit and the pleasure to be had from a command of a second language.

The possibility of personal contact with natives of other lands, either in this country or abroad, offers the primary reason for the study of foreign languages, in the opinion of Pete French, President, Pete French and Company. Mr. French, speaking from experience, adds: "To those students who are considering careers that will take them to foreign countries permanently or on trips, a basic knowledge of foreign languages is of prime importance and the opportunity afforded them during their college days should not be lost." In these days, when most men do not know when or in what capacity they will find themselves on foreign soil, even those students who have no thought of a career abroad may do well to heed the advice of Mr. French.

Too few people realize how many firms, big and little, now have contact with foreign markets, either to sell, or to buy. W. W. Gallagher, Jr., of the MacGregor Instrument Company, points up this fact: "Most of us are now in the foreign markets and it is essential that we have people familiar with our business who can discuss these matters in the tongue or language of the country concerned. . . . There is definitely a field in our industry for persons who have a knowledge of the industry . . . in combination with spoken and written language of one or more other countries, abroad in the world."

M. G. Garcia, Vice President and General Manager of the Kelly-Koett International Corporation, sends a statement in which he calls the opportunities in foreign trade for persons who possess foreign language skills "indeed excellent," but warns that "students must not be led to think, merely because they master Spanish, French, or any other commercial language, that the doors will automatically be opened to them."

The aviation industry obviously recognizes the importance of foreign languages for several different categories of employees. George Gardner, Educational Director of the Pan American World Airways

System, writes: "A knowledge of foreign languages is very necessary for several different categories of Pan American World Airways employees. The captains of the Clippers and the stewards and stewardesses must meet foreign language requirements and certain employees in the Traffic Department who work at the counter or otherwise come in contact with the public have use for foreign languages." Warren Lee Pierson, Chairman of the Board, Trans World Airline, writes that in his firm, which does business both in the United States and abroad, "a knowledge of foreign languages is useful in many positions and essential in some." William L. Griffith, Employment Manager, Eastern Airlines, mentions particularly an "International Desk," which his company maintains at major points of entry where the ability to speak a certain language is a requirement for the position.

The importance of foreign languages to research men is the concern of L. T. Hallet, Chairman, College Recruiting Committee, General Aniline and Film Corporation: "It is a definite asset that research and production men be able to read, and translate into English, German, French, and, in some cases, Russian technical articles."

The opinion of an executive in a field intimately concerned with communication is of particular interest. A. L. Hammell, President, Railway Express Agency, finds: "The world, however, is constantly growing smaller and I think as time goes on an understanding of some foreign languages—possibly Spanish and French—will be very helpful in the express business. In fact, some of our people, seeing the coming need for such understanding, are studying a foreign language at the present time."

H. A. Stanton, Vice President of the Norton Company, suggests that a student who intends to work in foreign countries should concentrate particularly on a fluent knowledge of French or Spanish, or both. The language combination mentioned is interesting, since the Norton Company has manufacturing branch plants in Australia, Canada, England, France, Germany, Italy, and selling arrangements in all the principal industrial markets in the world. Evidently French and Spanish are still dominant for practical commercial use. Incidentally, Mr. Stanton is critical of the normal achievement of a four-year college course in language. He finds it of doubtful value to a young American business man because of a common failure to perfect normal conversational use of the language.

The advantage held by the applicant trained in foreign languages over one not so trained is clearly indicated in the statement of Richard G. Hanna, Gray Marine Motor Company: "All other things being equal, unquestionably the person trained in foreign languages would be selected for a job over those not so equipped." Although sound business training plus a thorough understanding of foreign countries and their business take precedence over the ability to speak foreign languages, Mr. Hanna feels that when languages are added to these qualifications, the person is in an excellent position to "handle any job that comes along." The value of foreign languages in fashion merchandising is given a high place in the estimation of Henriette Hautefeuille, General Manager, Callot Soeurs of Paris, Inc.: "In fashion merchandising, a knowledge of foreign languages is becoming increasingly helpful. In this respect, a working knowledge of French is of great help, as well as the more commonly used school knowledge." This last sentence is significant, since "school knowledge" of French is obviously not considered a working knowledge.

The opportunity to use foreign language skills in highly attractive positions abroad should be of interest to many persons with banking experience or technical training. I do not mean persons just out of college, since the positions to which William M. Healy, Manager, Export Sales Department, Rheem Manufacturing Company, refers would be available only to persons of long experience and high qualifications. Mr. Healy writes: "The Rheem Manufacturing Company has had considerable experience recently in operations outside the continental limits of the United States. One of our problems has been the obtaining of properly qualified personnel to fill executive positions in our overseas plants, overseas offices, and conducting market surveys in the various markets in which we feel developments are of interest to us."

W. R. Herstein, Executive Director, Memphis International Center, reports that many manufacturers and shippers of the Memphis area have in their offices employees acquainted with at least one language other than English. Although the number of persons so employed may not be great in one urban center, the number of persons so employed in one area could be multiplied many times by the total number of manufacturing or distribution centers in the United States. The number of persons employed in office positions requiring knowledge of a foreign language must rise to a figure of formidable proportions.

Many of the persons added to an office force partly because of their knowledge of one or more foreign languages not only owe their job to the fact that they possess such knowledge, but they also receive a higher salary for the same reason. It is not generally known that a knowledge of a foreign language can and often does result in a higher salary rating. Estimates of how much the salary of the person trained in foreign languages may exceed the salary of persons in like positions without such training range from four to twenty-five per cent. The statement of James B. Herzog, President of Stern, Morgenthau and Company, is one of many showing such possibilities of higher salaries: "In practically every phase of our operations, an individual with a knowledge of one or more languages is in a preferred position. . . . I can safely say that such an accomplishment makes it possible for the individual to earn more money than if he or she were without it."

Since the claims just made have appeared very often in relation to technical and engineering positions, quite aside from positions in export work, I feel justified in saying that those students who add usable language skills to their technical training will open for themselves new fields of opportunity and attractive salary ratings which might not otherwise be available. While this may not be true in every case, the better salary and greater opportunities for advancement would seem to be highly probable in the light of the information received. Certainly, administrators in technical and engineering schools should reconsider the unimportant place now given to foreign languages in their curricula.

The ever increasing opportunities for engineers trained in foreign languages, and for technically and linguistically trained persons, in foreign operations have been either too little known, or completely ignored. No other conclusion is possible when we examine the true nature of the unimportant place given foreign languages in technical preparation of almost every kind. The following statement, one of 153 of essentially the same general import, should offer ample food for thought. J. K. Jenny, Assistant Director, Foreign Relations Department, E. I. du Pont de Nemours and Company, points out that the du Pont foreign organization must place first in importance the necessary business or technical background of the person employed, so as to bring the particular type of experience developed in American industry into the foreign field, but says further: "If such men are to be successful they must have or acquire language qualifications and an understanding of the customs of the country to which they are assigned and the mentality of the people thereof. Obviously, if men have both sets of qualifications their opportunities for selection and advancement in the foreign field are much greater than others who only have the necessary vocational qualifications. . . . Young men who can add to the requisite technical education a knowledge of languages, history, etc., are very much in demand for foreign job opportunities." G. S.

Joy, Office Manager, Libby, McNeill and Libby, is one of many who agree with Mr. Jenny's estimate of the value of such a combination, although without particular reference to employment abroad.

In our examination of the importance of foreign languages to engineering and technical students, the statement of General Brehon Somervell, now President of the Koppers Company, Inc., is particularly pertinent, in that it touches on both the immediate, practical importance of language skills and the broad cultural contributions of such study. I quote only briefly from his longer analysis of the present state of technical preparation. He believes that if engineers "are to have a broad cultural background they must necessarily know some of the languages of other nations. German has long been considered an essential for those interested in the sciences, in which Germany has excelled. Some understanding of the romance languages would seem to be necessary. In our own case we are in daily need of a working knowledge of German, French and Spanish."

Many schools of commerce have come to consider foreign languages so unimportant that they have dropped all foreign language requirements. They may well take note of the great number of commercial positions which require the use of foreign languages. The information received indicates a growing need for more foreign language study in combinations with commercial courses. To mention only one aspect of the situation, the ever-growing field of opportunity for persons with secretarial skills, in combination with foreign language skills and a knowledge of foreign areas, is being seriously slighted. The remarks of H. S. Hower, Jr., Manager, Corning Glass Works, are representative of those received about stenographers: "We have within our organization a definite need for people with a fluent speaking, writing, and reading knowledge of French, German, Spanish, and Portuguese. These people are classified as Foreign Language Stenographers."

Mr. Hower's recognition of the importance of language skills to sales personnel in his firm is also typical of replies concerning the importance of languages to salesmen whose duties do not necessarily include direct foreign contact: "While the knowledge of a foreign language is not essential in any of our sales positions, it is interesting to note that, at least, 80 per cent of our sales personnel have taken time and expended the effort to obtain at least a smattering of one or more languages either through organized study or individually at home."

In a letter which stresses the value to business personnel of foreign language training as a part of a liberal education, E. Kriegsman, President, Kriegsman Paper Company, concludes: "I firmly believe that such a liberal education would be incomplete without a working knowledge of at least one modern foreign language. I believe that it is a necessity in this shrinking world to understand the thoughts and philosophies of people from other countries and that this can best be done by talking to those people and reading their literature in their own language."

In hundreds of letters, the theme of the importance and the practical utility of foreign languages has been enriched by continually recurring expressions of faith in the value, for the individual and society, of carrying language study to a level which guarantees real understanding, so that the individual can profit fully from readings in foreign literatures and from a consideration of the mental, artistic and national characteristics of peoples of foreign nations.

John J. McCarthy, Assistant General Manager, Gimbel Brothers, New York, feels that it is especially important for business and for the nation to prepare more business executives to understand and sympathize with other cultures. Such understanding will be acquired through the language and cultural products of foreign nations. Writing as one not directly engaged in foreign operations, but as one who is very close to the many human problems of a large department store, Mr. McCarthy says: "Obviously, the study of *any* foreign language has a pronounced effect, for the good, on one's English. Furthermore, the intelligent study of any foreign language includes a study of the culture of the nation involved, and this has a pronounced broadening effect upon the student. If there is one thing we need in business today, it is executives who have grown to the point where they are catholic in their interests, and *understanding,* not merely tolerant of other people's mores, moods and actions."

Some business men have expressed the belief that the practical value of language and liberal arts subjects will continue to be demonstrated in the future. A typical comment is that of J. F. McCrudden, Export Manager, Aberfoyle Manufacturing Company, "It is the opinion of the writer that effective study of such liberal arts subjects as language, including English, are at the present time highly important, and we believe that there will be no change in such requirements during the next five or ten years. We believe that the standard that will be required of those engaged in business will require a full knowledge of at least one foreign language." Not only is there a widespread opinion that the need for such knowledge will continue, but there are also frequent suggestions that it will increase. Walter P. Marshall, President, Western Union Telegraph Company, asserts:

"I venture the opinion . . . that there will be increasing need for such knowledge in this country generally, as the operations of the North Atlantic Pact and the pressure of the situation abroad have their impact on our economy generally."

The importance of foreign languages with regard to international understanding is brought out in the letter of the president of an important manufacturing firm, who asked that his name be withheld. He maintains that a speaking and reading knowledge of foreign languages is likely to prove valuable as the participation of the United States grows in world affairs. In his opinion, "this participation is essential to our national well being. Therefore, it is reasonable to expect that the education and training in French, Spanish, and German may open many doors of opportunity that otherwise will be closed to young men in the immediate future."

Even persons employed in domestic sales work, who have no expectation of going into the foreign branch of a firm, may find themselves chosen for advancement in rank and in responsibility—with attendant increases in salary—because of their knowledge of language. The reason is that they are potential replacements for the rapidly expanding foreign divisions of their firm. William L. Neilson, Jr., Export Manager, Greenfield Tap and Die Corporation, explains it this way: "Young men entering the company's employment in a sales capacity would receive some preference because of language skills since this would give us potential replacements for the export position." The practice of hiring sales personnel for work in domestic markets with a view to their possible transfer later to sales work involving foreign markets is not unusual among firms having foreign business.

Max L. Pilliard, Baz-Dresch, Pilliard and Company, International Trade Consultants, offers the following statement concerning the important role of foreign languages in business today: "For the aggressive businessman of today and the future, I would say that it is not only necessary but understood that he will have a conversational knowledge of at least two languages in addition to English." The letters on file reveal strong support for the idea that the aggressive business man of today who has contact with foreign buying and selling needs two or more foreign languages in his work and that the business man of the future may find a knowledge of several foreign languages an asset well worth the time, energy, and money which such preparation may require. Mr. Pilliard goes on to say: "A language could be compared to a piano player who has learned his scales or arpeggios prior to being a concert master. He certainly could not give a concert by playing the scales on the piano, but they are a necessity for his being able to present a masterful piano performance." The figure is particularly apt, for, just as the scales on a piano do not directly make the material of a concert, or justify the salary paid the concert master, so do foreign languages alone fail to assure adequate performance in business matters or attractive salaries in the business world. Yet without a background of foreign language study, adequate performance may be impossible and advancement to more attractive salaries may not be realized.

The increasing contact of the modern business establishment with foreign buyers is the theme of a statement by George S. Pillsbury, Overseas Vice President, Pillsbury Mills, Inc.: "In our firm we also, of course, pay a great deal of attention to foreign languages, because many of our buyers speak no English. Thus it is essential that their own language be known by the various members of our firm."

Foreign languages are important to employers and their firms, as well as to prospective employees. Having employees adequately prepared in foreign languages is good business and can very well mean improved business relations, more efficient conduct of business, and more orders. Clarence O. Swanson, Treasurer, Commerce Oil Corporation, points out the utility of languages used to such purposes: "There is no doubt in our minds . . . that if we could reply to all our customers in their own language, it would improve customer relations and would perhaps result in more orders when business again becomes competitive." Whether Mr. Swanson has found it so or not, other letters of reply pointed out that, much as they would like to improve business relations by dealing with customers in their own language, this is not usually possible. The reason is simple: they are unable to find and hire persons who offer a satisfactory combination of business ability and skill in the use of foreign languages. This is a result of failure to train such persons in the nation's educational program. In addition, blame can be placed on ignorance of the fact that firms which we regularly consider domestic in their interest have broad foreign contacts, both in buying and in selling. Not enough people know that there are few firms of any size which do not have, or plan to have, profitable business relations with foreign areas.

Foreign languages are of peculiar value in the field of publishing. Yet, as the writers of more than one third of the letters insist, the vocational value of foreign language study, great as it may be, is far exceeded by its contribution to the development of a clear-thinking, cultured individual. B. H. Walton, of the firm of Allyn and Bacon, is one of the many to express this view: "As is so often the case in school studies in general, language training contributes so greatly to the development of the pupil into a cultured individual that this value may exceed any immediate vocational value that the study may have."

The point of view of the newspaper publisher is also of interest. Eugene Meyer, publisher of the *Washington Post,* feels that not enough people are learning languages: "I am afraid not enough people are being educated in this country in foreign languages, a knowledge which I consider essential for reporters and our diplomatic and commercial foreign representatives."

Skills in the use of language are of real and potential value to the social worker, especially in urban and industrial centers. In port cities, they are frequently indispensable. Gladys E. Townsend, Director of Services, The Travelers Aid Society of New York, writes on this subject: "Any language facility which our workers or volunteers have is frequently called into use. . . . For casework positions in our Port Department facility in speaking at least one language in addition to English is required." Social workers in large urban centers, where there are heavy concentrations of persons who speak foreign languages, are also expected to know at least one language in addition to English. In fact, persons working in social and welfare services generally find that they have need for language skills.

Argus Tresidder, Director of Communications, Joseph E. Seagram and Sons, Inc., offers interesting comment of a former teacher who is now serving in industry: "I feel that in the growing international interdependence there is going to be greater and greater need of language ability. Many of our employees, for example, want opportunities to continue their study abroad. Most are balked by the requirement that they speak another language than English. . . . I was for many years a college teacher in the field of the humanities. Naturally I believe in the importance of such studies in the advancement of the individual, whatever his professional aim." The importance of language to the technical employee who may wish to improve himself through technical study abroad is yet another evidence of the versatile utility of languages.

The field of opportunity for personnel trained in languages to conduct tours abroad is an obvious one. On the other hand, in the home offices, located in this country, someone must carry on the large amount of correspondence which must be handled in many languages. B. W. Van Riper, Educational Travel Division, American Express Company, reports: "Certainly we have men in the office here who can carry on correspondence in all the important languages." In order to find fully qualified personnel, the company prefers those who have lived in the foreign country for some length of time.

A few executives express the opinion that foreign language study should begin early in life. Among these is Vaughn M. Bryant, Publicity Director for International House, New Orleans, who writes: "My personal view is that the study of language in our school system could not be stressed too much. My only complaint is that I believe such instruction should be started in the second and third grades in conversational methods and not be withheld until the child has passed that useful period when the learning of new languages and new words comes easily to him."

Speaking for the company which he heads, William C. White, President of the Alcoa Steamship Company, Inc., says: "We in this country do not stress languages enough in our general education scheme. I would like to see every college force every liberal arts student to take four years of written English and four years of Oral English as well as foreign language. . . . A foreign language will broaden any man and be helpful in his general education. Spanish is the major foreign language spoken in the territory served by our vessels and the ability to speak Spanish would be an advantage for any of our employees." James B. Young, Vice President of the Barber Steamship Lines, Inc., agrees with Mr. White in considering foreign languages of special value in the shipping business: "In the steamship business, knowledge of foreign languages would, of course, be of considerable help to one who is engaged in it and would, in my opinion, be a strong point in favor of one applying for a position in the industry. I suggest Spanish, French, Norwegian and Japanese."

That a need exists in governmental activities abroad for more trained specialists who know the language of the area in which they serve is evident from the statement by Lucius D. Clay, General, Retired, U. S. Army: "The great increase in our governmental activities abroad has increased the demand for competent persons who speak foreign languages fluently. I would like to emphasize that the latter requirement is in addition to technical competence and does not compensate for lack of training and ability in other fields. We were constantly handicapped in Germany because our well trained specialists could not speak German. . . . Salaries for governmental positions requiring knowledge of foreign languages range from $4,000 to $12,000 a year."

Special attention is given in the Appendix to the replies of persons in government, but a few brief quotations from these letters will show the trend. J. C. Green, Executive Director, Board of Examiners for the Foreign Service, writes that "a reading ability of at least one of five specified modern languages is a requirement for appointment as Foreign Service Officer." Nathan Habib, Chief, Shipping Statistics Section, Foreign Trade Division, Bureau of Census, assures me that "languages are indispensable in the field of international economics, foreign trade, and transportation." Eldon P. King, Special Deputy Commissioner, Bureau of Internal Revenue, relates the ability to use foreign languages to the international aspect of his work: "In this field . . . a command over one or more additional languages is of considerable value." The attitudes expressed by governmental executives are quite as favorable toward foreign languages as those expressed by business men.

But the voice of the American business man, so potent in many quarters, finds little echo in academic halls. In spite of the favorable attitude of men at the higher managerial levels toward language study, American colleges and universities, especially the business and engineering divisions, show in this respect a lamentable lack of foresight in preparing students for their future life work. Preparatory schools and high schools must also share the blame for sending forth graduates who are virtually ignorant of languages other than their own. The pressing needs of the day, in business, industry and government, make more urgent, in the view of many executives, a program that will strongly implement technical knowledge with a sound knowledge of foreign languages and cultures. Certainly the time has come for educators speedily to fill the present educational gaps with thorough-going courses in language.

IV

OPPORTUNITIES FOR EMPLOYMENT
AND SUGGESTED COURSE
COMBINATIONS

THERE IS ONLY ONE dependable source of information concerning the nature, location and number of vocational opportunities for persons who have foreign language skills, and that is the adequately informed person within the employing firm. Since the person who does the employing must keep in mind the attitude of his superiors and company policy, I made every effort to canvass the opinion and attitude of the highest executives, as well as those who have direct contacts with the job candidates. The second question of my letter-questionnaire reflects my respect for the long and successful experience of the typical executive.

In view of your personal experience, and your knowledge of your firm, what opportunities exist for persons trained in foreign languages?

By the nature of the question, the way was left open for the representative to report opportunities known to him, whether they existed in his own company or not. The quantity of pertinent information acquired by use of this question exceeds by far the information which company policy would permit the executives to reveal.

A great many executives were good enough to send—not always for publication—a large amount of specific information concerning job opportunities and company needs which would be of interest to prospective applicants. My letter assured all recipients that the request for information about openings was not for the purpose of directing applicants to them. Thus, some of the most interesting and significant information is not available for publication. Nevertheless, such information will play an important part in the development of this study and the conclusions drawn from it.

Before a list of fields and vocations reported as areas of opportunity for students adequately prepared in foreign languages is presented, it may be useful to name areas of demand which, more than others, are favorable to foreign language students seeking employment. A statistical count of replies which mention fields of opportunity yields the following results.

In the 206 replies to the second question of the basic letter, three fields were mentioned far more often than any others. First in order is *management*. Next is *foreign trade*. This category includes all phases of world trade, export and import, with numerous positions listed as available both here and abroad. Third in order is the field of *sales*, with the emphasis upon work in this country relating to sales abroad, and upon work involving direct contact with all phases of sales and marketing in foreign areas. In the order of preference, other fields which were most frequently mentioned are: *engineering and technical positions, positions in the federal government, advertising, journalism and public relations, secretarial positions, translating and interpreting,* and *positions in transportation, banking and finance, accounting, statistics, market analysis, radio and television.*

The fields just named are only the leaders in a list of more than one hundred fields and vocations representing opportunities for employment suggested by the letters. Too long to be included at this point, the list is contained in the Appendix.

Even if some allowance is made for overlapping, the distribution of the kinds of business, industrial, or vocational opportunity is broad enough to indicate clearly that demand for persons trained in foreign languages exists in practically every major division of American business and industry and in the various departments of the Federal government. More than 250 job types are reported in all fields.

While a specific numerical estimate of the demand for language-trained persons is not offered here, the information received leads to the inference that the total demand far exceeds the supply. Indeed, it would appear that the shortage of persons who offer adequate background in language study is so acute that many business and governmental activities cannot be brought to a state of full efficiency and economy of operation until more persons are properly trained and made available. Support for this statement will be found in the analyses of jobs and areas of demand which are to be found in the Appendix. In view of the number of kinds of employment in which language skills and abilities are valuable, it would appear that foreign language studies have a real financial and generally utilitarian value.

Since so many persons contributed detailed answers to the question about the courses and course combinations which may lead to success in different fields of endeavor, it is not possible to give here the detail received concerning the suggested combinations of studies. However, it is possible to indicate the essential characteristics of the high school and undergraduate college curricula suggested by experienced persons in direct contact with the educational needs of business and government. The question which prompted the response described here was:

If we assume that personal qualifications are favorable, what special studies, or course combinations, will offer the best chances of success in the positions you have in mind?

In their general aspect, the answers to this question could be summarized as follows. Out of 200 letters which offer details concerning preferred courses and course combinations, 150 list subjects in the humanities, with English (language, literature and speech), foreign languages, cultural products of foreign areas, and history being most frequently mentioned. The suggested content of courses in American history and in the history of foreign areas was often extended to include foreign relations and economic background. Various branches of economics, and economic geography in particular, received much favorable comment. The same letters which list courses falling under the general heading of the humanities also use the general term "liberal arts" to refer to the courses which offer the best chances of success in the positions reported.

The trend of the replies was clearly toward a curriculum in high school and in college which has as its core language, literature, history, economics, and geography. Presumably, courses in mathematics and the sciences would also receive some emphasis. Accounting received strong support. In other words, the traditional subjects of the liberal arts program are held to be the courses which—as a foundation of general education on which specialization is to be built—offer the best chances of success in the wide variety of positions reported.

The preferred courses for technical and commercial schools, and for programs of specialized study built on the foundation of liberal studies, assumed the following pattern. Out of the two hundred letters which answered the question, 134 named engineering, or a branch thereof, as the course offering the best chance of success in jobs which were of special interest to persons skilled in the use of foreign languages. This number was far in excess of the 68 for foreign trade (international trade regulations, traffic, documents, etc.), the 62 for business administration, the 48 for accounting (public utility accounting, etc.), the 36 for banking and finance, the 28 for chemistry, and the 26 for salesmanship. The trend of the numerical count and remarks in a number of letters support the idea that technical skills and foreign language skills offer the most favorable combination for lucrative employment. The combination of commercial studies and foreign languages also finds much favor but does not offer quite as many opportunities, presumably because of the greater amount of competition already existing in the commercial field.

The large amount of detail received concerning the value of area studies and other specialized programs cannot properly be included here. I can say, however, that specialized study was generally presented in the letters of reply as belonging to the graduate level, or to part-time study programs.

Perhaps the significance of the information offered in this chapter lies not only in the kind of studies offering the best chances of success in business, industry and government, but also in the simplicity of the curriculum suggested. Certainly the basic curriculum of language, literature, history, economics, accounting, geography, mathematics and some studies in the sciences, would be a model of simplicity if it were compared to the long list of courses comprising the curriculum of the liberal arts college, or even of the large high school.

V

THE LIBERAL ARTS AND
THE HUMANITIES

CLAIMS HAVE BEEN MADE, and most often by professors of the liberal
arts, that the humanities afford the best training of the mind, and
therefore of the individual, for the higher intellectual tasks. What do
the business executives say on these matters? Do they agree with the
liberal arts professors?

Before reporting what the business executives say, I quote again
from the basic letter. The first sentence reads: "I am preparing an
analysis of the views of business executives and industrialists concerning the value of liberal arts training in general and foreign language studies in particular, especially as a part of a preparation for
employment in business and industry." The first question ran thus:

> What relative importance for success in your field do you
> attach to effective study of such liberal arts subjects as lan-
> guage, including English, and the cultural products of foreign
> nations?

The original intention was to use the word "humanities," instead
of the term "liberal arts." Since most of the letters of reply use the
words "liberal arts" in the sense in which I would have used the word
"humanities," that is, referring to language and cultural studies without
special reference to the inclusion of science, I could have written this
chapter under the title of "Business, Government and the Humanities,"
instead of the present title. Of course, the conception of the humanities
presented here grants full recognition to science as the companion of
the humanities.

Behind the planning of this survey is the idea that the employer,
better than anyone else, knows the kind of preparation which he
wants prospective employees to have. Therefore, if we wish to learn
what business needs, we do not ask students, or parents of students, or
even inexperienced business men who have not had an opportunity to
know the field. I therefore approached a large number of persons

whose long experience, successful service, and level of present executive duties permit them to take the broad view in offering advice. Many teachers of cultural subjects, many school administrators, and many students—to say nothing of the general public—may expect these practical men to give a small, unimportant place to liberal arts subjects in the preparation of persons for business and technical jobs. That the effective study of such liberal arts subjects as language, including English, and the cultural products of foreign nations, has, in the opinion of men of action and achievement, an important contribution to make to chances for success in business and technical pursuits may be quite unexpected.

Eighty per cent of the employers who answered the question favored the liberal arts in general, and the humanities in particular, as the best preparation for the best jobs. This is to say that 274 of the 343 letters which answered the question about the importance of foreign languages and the liberal arts, speak favorably of the latter as important, essential, or as the best basic preparation for any job, including those of a business or technical nature. Of these 274 letters, which represent a wide sampling of American business and governmental executives, 108 went into some detail in their remarks on the value of liberal training. It is interesting to note that the letters which were most unequivocal in their favorable statements on this subject came primarily from executives at the highest levels. It would seem that the estimate of the necessity and value of an education in the humanities rises steadily as the individual climbs the executive ladder to places of responsibility and authority. On the other hand, the percentage given above shows that many executives at the lower levels are also aware of these same values. The quotations offered in this chapter are meant to be representative of all groups. As in other parts of this study the answers in this chapter assume that at least a minimum of business or technical competence is necessary to obtain a business or technical job and to be successful in it.

Irving S. Olds, Chairman of the Board of Directors, United States Steel Corporation, in a second letter concerning this survey, enclosed a letter from H. J. Phillips, Jr., Organization Planning Supervisor, United States Steel Corporation of Delaware, as part of his answer to my questions. Mr. Phillips' letter is a good point of departure for a discussion of balance between liberal arts subjects and technical subjects: "I believe that the man's need for the two types shifts considerably as he advances in business. In his early years he can make best use of fairly practical technical subjects. As he advances in management, he is more concerned with broad economic and social considerations. . . . It is my personal opinion that a young man should follow a broad curriculum with just enough specialization in his preferred field to confirm his interest in it as a career; and, secondly, to permit him to meet technical requirements during his first few years out of college. It is comparatively easy to acquire specialized education on a postgraduate basis. The lines of least resistance will cause an individual to study in his specialized field rather than in the liberal arts field." The materials enclosed by Mr. Phillips emphasize the desirability of a reasonably liberal college curriculum rather than maximum specialization in a specialized field. The following opening remarks in material describing requirements for industrial accounting careers in U. S. Steel illustrate this preference: "The chief qualifying factors in employing college graduates for development as future industrial accounting and management men are capacity for development, personality and sufficient preliminary educational background to comprehend basic problems encountered in the training program. Our objective is to acquire men with management potentialities, rather than merely good technical ability." It is obvious from this last sentence that "merely good technical ability" is not enough.

Again and again the replies showed that the executive thinks that the person who is trained only in specific skills, only in practice, is at the mercy of the rapid shifts in emphasis and technique of the modern world. The man who understands the principle, the one who has the broad, flexible approach to be gained only from the liberal arts, is presented as the best prepared candidate for a position, the one in greatest demand. One employer, for example, makes the statement, with reference to assignments as foreign sales representatives, that his firm could not use specialists in such positions because of the very broad range of duties involved. In the same way, this limitation is reported as being applicable in varying degrees to many domestic positions.

Business is so varied in requirement today that a broad educational background seems to be necessary for any person who would serve his company well. The increasing demands of business are making the narrow specialist less valuable.

Let us consider now some of the facts reported by R. J. Aitchison, President, Fansteel Metallurgical Corporation: "Our business happens to comprise an assortment of extremely technical products which requires a large number of technicians and trained workers in a number of specialized fields. Perhaps this is why I feel so keenly that too many over-emphasize the 'speciality' and 'technical' features and forget the importance of clear thinking and sound reasoning of just 'ordinary horse sense.'" In the opinion of Mr. Aitchison, "Any series of studies which promotes the general ability of the student to think clearly and analyze carefully, must be of sound eventual value to that student. . . . Of course one must understand figures and the import of relations which are expressed in ratios and figures. Of course one must understand something of the natural expectancies of human actions and reactions. Of course one must have some basic training in language and expression. Of course one must cover a sufficient variety of studies and training to develop a personal understanding and a personality which will wear well with a majority of people he comes in contact with. Fundamentally one must acquire the ability to adapt his knowledge and understanding to the position he fills, and most of all, develop sufficiently sound logical reasoning powers to carry that note of conviction so necessary if others are to do as directed and do it wholeheartedly." Mr. Aitchison sums up his views this way: "Therefore my personal feeling about college courses is not so much from the angle of specializing in any one subject or group of subjects but rather from the standpoint that the college courses are mental exercises designed to expand the thinking and reasoning and analytical ability of the student."

If one takes into account the widespread dissatisfaction expressed concerning the graduates of our schools, it seems quite possible that the broad understanding which only the liberal arts can give is not sufficiently available to the American student. The last sentence of Mr. Aitchison's letter adds to my long list of revealing critical statements: "I feel very strongly on the foregoing convictions because the more you talk to applicants and seekers of good positions the more one realizes the lack of broad understanding in so many people whose academic background should have accomplished more."

I have quoted at some length from Mr. Aitchison's letter because his letter is typical of the point of view expressed in many other letters. Other statements included here will show that this is not an isolated expression of the primary nature of the role of the liberal arts in any preparation for business. There is the letter of Edward L. Ryerson, Chairman of the Board, Inland Steel Company: "On the basis of the broadest interpretation of the educational requirements that would be of most value, I would certainly include a provision requiring a comprehensive study of the liberal arts, and this may or may not include foreign languages, depending upon what other alternatives may be offered to obtain a broad liberal education." Although Houlder Hudgins, President, Sloane-Blabon Corporation, finds that the experience of results attained by individuals is based more on their qualities than the nature of their training, he does say: "Except for the procurement of technical members of our staff, such as chemists, physicists, and engineers, we have found that the graduates of Liberal Arts courses succeed as well in our commercial departments as those trained in Business Schools." This observation is commonly made by executives who have observed the performance of graduates of specialized programs as they work, side by side, with persons having liberal arts training.

Along with many other executives, Warren Lee Pierson, Chairman of the Board, Trans World Airlines, believes that "in general some familiarity with the liberal arts is essential to enjoyment of life and to well-balanced participation in any field of endeavor." Edward J. Noble, Chairman of the Board, American Broadcasting Company, Inc., says: "There is no question that a broad education in the liberal arts is of real value to men and women who plan to enter the business world. It is no guarantee of success, but certainly many individuals find their futures enhanced by some knowledge of foreign countries and their business and cultural affairs. . . . With regard to technical and scientific skills, it is of course essential that people who will engage in the technical aspects of broadcasting be thoroughly prepared to do so. But few men, as they have advanced in their chosen fields of occupation, regret such broad backgrounds in the arts as they may have acquired during the early years. I would encourage any young man or woman to take full advantage of these opportunities during the college years." This is not an isolated bit of advice, since hundreds of executives suggested, directly or in effect, the same thing. For example, Elliott M. Sanger, Executive Vice President, WQXR and WQXR-FM, Radio Stations of *The New York Times,* points out that in a station which, like WQXR, specializes in good music and programs of a higher cultural level, a background of English, foreign languages and the liberal arts is essential in all departments. Mr. Sanger closes with these words: "In the field of radio, I would say that the wider your knowledge and background, the more likely you are to succeed."

Walter P. Marshall, President, The Western Union Telegraph Company, says that "technical and scientific skills are necessarily of great importance in the field of communications, but I should not wish to minimize for a moment the need for and value of a thorough basic background in the liberal arts, no matter what added professional, scientific or other specialized knowledge may then have to be taught or acquired." In like manner, many other executives suggest technical or scientific training should not precede a thorough grounding in the liberal arts.

H. Carl Wolf, Managing Director of the American Gas Association, offers the following remarks, both general and specific: "It is my view that colleges should educate students to be citizens, to get full enjoyment out of life and to know how to acquire specialized training. I believe that industry should pick college graduates who have good basic education, the ability to think and the ability to learn, and train them for their special purposes." Mr. Wolf, in his conception of education, would include languages, both foreign and English, "because they help a person think and also because they are necessary if we are to acquire the ability to adequately express our views to others." He would include cultural and economic problems of foreign nations as vital, "inasmuch as life in our own country is so intimately bound up with that in other parts of the world." He would stress political and economic studies which would tend to show the differences between the American system, which has proved so successful, and all other political and ideological systems. But, all in all, he "would lay stress on teaching how to think rather than attempting to burden a student with the details which after all have more to do with training and experience." R. E. Woodruff, President, Erie Railroad Company, after expressing his feeling as to the beneficial effects of Latin for understanding, as well as his feeling that foreign language skills were too specialized to rank high in qualifications for employment in railroading, goes on to say: "We lay much more stress, however, on a study on the part of engineering students of some of the things you call the humanities. . . ."

R. L. White, Treasurer of the Tennessee Eastman Corporation, says: "The primary benefit in industry of any foreign language training, excluding the ability to translate a particular language, is the wider range of thought and understanding which that training brings to problems arising in the course of work. From what I have observed, the whole purpose of liberal arts training is to stimulate one's natural curiosity and increase one's knowledge of how to live, how to meet others and enjoy those contacts in everyday life." An executive in one of our largest companies, who prefers not to be mentioned, helps round out this same idea: "In general we like to see a man's college courses cover a fairly broad field; we like to see him take courses which require the use of original thinking and analysis rather than the memorizing of facts and text book opinions; we like courses which require a considerable amount of writing and oral exposition, so that a man learns to express himself clearly and concisely in talking and in writing."

A person of prominence in the financial world, who prefers to remain anonymous, has—in my opinion—written so well on the subject under examination that I quote him here at length:

"I feel that the value of a college education is not to be measured in terms of information acquired (a purely mechanical process of memory), but rather in the study habits developed and the broad point of view that stems therefrom. The needs of business are primarily for people who can dig for information, evaluate the data when obtained, think through to a logical conclusion for a course of action, and express their conclusions in clear and intelligent English prose. These elements can be acquired in a Liberal Arts course. All colleges recognize the importance of physical education to keep the muscles flexed and the body channels open. The analogy applies with an equal emphasis to the mind. The mental gymnastics of wrapping the mind around algebraic formulae, the declensions of Latin nouns, or the conjugation of French verbs serves to produce a suppleness of the mental process which does not deteriorate with the same rapidity as age brings to the physical process.

"Beyond the purely mental calisthenic aspect of such studies is the fact that a Liberal Arts course ordinarily exposes the student to either the political or the cultural history of at least one nation and places before his views the parade of centuries of development of thought, philosophy, history and culture. It is this latter experience which serves to make the businessman of the future a person who can do the afore-mentioned job of evaluating facts, of thinking them through to the logical conclusion, and beyond that, adjusting the facts to the personal characteristics which still pervade all business relationships.

"Thus, I feel that the broadening influence of a Liberal Arts course is invaluable and I feel that the study habits developed can be applied to the post-college process of acquiring specific technical knowledge needed for a given job in a chosen field of endeavor."

John N. McDonnell, Vice President, Schering Corporation, adds the following thought based on his own experience: "Our particular field happens to be that of research in, and the manufacture, promotion, and marketing of prescription pharmaceuticals, proprietary medication, and cosmetic products. In this field, collegiate study in liberal arts subjects can be considered a most important prerequisite." Mr. McDonnell considers English literature the nucleus of a liberal education, and contact with the wisdom of the outstanding writers of the past a necessary part of such education. Beyond English and foreign literatures, he would stress economics, sociology, and psychology.

B. L. Babcock, Treasurer, Endicott Johnson Corporation, offers advice drawn from his own experience: "It happens that I have both an A.B. and a LL.B. Degree. Of the courses leading to these degrees the liberal arts work has been the more valuable to me. My son who has recently graduated from High School is entering College this fall. He wants to go into business. To be properly prepared for it he is following the advice of his father that he attend a liberal arts college four years before going to business school. It is much more important that he do so today than it was a generation ago. Without the cultural training that one receives from liberal arts subjects I feel that he would always be under a handicap even in business." The preceding letter is merely one example of a prevalent idea. The dominating note of the replies is that it is today more important for a business person to have a broad background of liberal arts training prior to specialization than it was a generation ago. An employee has less and less chance of rising to a high place in business simply on the basis of experience. Experience alone is no longer enough, since the complexities of business today require far more intelligence, knowledge, imagination, and breadth of formal educational contact than did the business world of twenty or thirty years ago.

Roger Albright, Director of Educational Services, Motion Picture Association of America, Inc., points out that he had conversations and conferences with various people in the motion picture industry. The reactions "seem to indicate a general high regard for liberal arts training." In more detail, he writes: "A principal contribution of the liberal arts college is that it is a training ground where many students learn how to learn. This learning skill is, of course, very valuable for those who go on to technical schools, but it is also valuable to those who assume responsibilities not requiring scientific skills. A general observation is that many who have had the experience of a liberal arts college acquire skills and facilities in non-technical routines more readily than if they had not had the liberal arts college experience." To continue with the answer of Mr. Albright, which presumably represents the opinion of many others in the motion picture industry: "Increasingly, liberal arts college curricula establish certain cultural interests which are always welcome, particularly with executive personnel. Such persons are always able to think and live with a better balance of life interest than those whose only area of intensive experience is in the grooves of their livelihood. Unfortunately, the liberal arts college seems to be the main source of balanced life interests."

John T. Schenck, President, The Engelberg Huller Co., Inc., is of the opinion that "a liberal arts training is the best basic education in any field of endeavor, as those so equipped seem to have a broader vision and a better understanding of all arts and sciences than those whose education has been limited to specific fields." Archie Lochhead, President, Universal Trading Corporation, feels that if a student has no special field in mind, "a broad liberal arts course intensive enough to train his mind in independent thinking is the best recommendation." An executive who permits publication, provided I do not reveal the source, sends the following remarks, which could well have been made by a professor of the humanities: "The only importance that I, as an individual, attach to the study of foreign languages, is the personal satisfaction that it must bring to those who realize that linguistic ability lays open before them a world of knowledge and understanding; a world beyond the reach of those who lack the equipment to receive, at first hand, the cultural advantages that other nations have to offer." The same letter continues with these words, almost of warning: "Speaking strictly from the commercial viewpoint, I fear that, as long as international relations are fostered only to the degree that an inherently isolationist mentality is prepared to pay it lip service, the value of linguistic training will continue to be measured in terms of cultural achievement, rather than dollars and cents."

The importance of liberal arts training to engineers is summarized well in the following words of Bryant Essick, President of Essick Manufacturing Company: "For final success in my field—the manufacturing of construction equipment and evaporative air coolers—I place a large degree of importance on some liberal arts training. . . . A young man entering my business will at first find himself so busy learning technical details that his liberal arts training, whatever it may have been, will seem entirely wasted. At the earlier levels of responsibility this will be largely true; but, as his job begins to expand to broader responsibilities, he will find that, no matter how technically expert he may be, without a good command of English and without some knowledge of the other liberal arts, he will not go ahead as readily as a second man who has both the technical background and a balance of at least the liberal arts which I recommend. . . . Certainly in my opinion the man or woman who is trained exclusively in the liberal arts or in technical and vocational courses will find it very difficult to rise above an average level of success, either in this business or in their home life. For better than average success there must be a balance of the two."

Mr. Essick's reminder of the value of technical subjects to a person with a liberal arts training seems most appropriate here. Yet, if both kinds of preparation are to be made available to the graduates of our schools, more time must be allowed for such studies. If one is to achieve better than average success, either in business or in home life, more time must be spent in formal education. There would seem to be little choice for the ambitious person. Furthermore, if the additional time pays sufficient financial dividends, as my information leads me to believe it does, the additional investment in time, energy and money will be worth while.

Henry W. Francis, Vice President, Francis Metal Products Company, another executive in the technical field, considers liberal arts training "not only as an asset but as a requisite to the well-equipped business or professional man or woman. Purely technical study does not provide the broader technique required for the fullest personal returns from business or professional experience nor to the successful processing of a life as a whole."

J. Holmes, answering for Harold H. Swift, President of Swift and Company, feels that the primary purpose of a college education is very different from that of the supporters of technical specialization at the undergraduate level: "I think that in approaching this problem, one must bear in mind that the prime purpose of a college education is to develop and stimulate the faculty for sound reasoning. A liberal arts course will provide this as well as any other course. The application of this ability to reason is a training job for the specific firm with which the individual becomes associated and cannot be acquired in a college course."

The technical preparation possible in the schoolroom has its limitations. The following letter from Kendall A. Redfield, President, The Asgrow Export Corporation, offers a good case in point: "In latter years, I am much more impressed with the necessity for including liberal arts subjects such as languages, including English, philosophy, etc., in modern curricula, even than those having to do with preparing students for technical work. My background is technical and I was educated to be an electrical engineer, and at the same time I was so busy studying precise scientific subjects that there was no time for languages or cultural subjects. I think that is a mistake. Of course it is elementary that no school can prepare a man completely for a given job. About the best an electrical engineering course, for example, can give a man is a good basis for learning many specifics which he will have to learn in whatever job he finds himself after school."

The letter of Irving J. Fain, Secretary, Apex Tire and Rubber Company, sheds further light on executive opinion: "To begin with, I have always had a strong prejudice in favor of non-vocational subjects as good, in fact, the best preparation for effective high level business success. In world trade, we operate often in an inexact field with vague knowledge, with frequent calls for judgment based on vague information of a varied and amorphous nature wherein the essence is that element of common sense, rather than statistical accuracy." The conditions mentioned here for those working in world trade have their counterparts in much of the domestic business world as well, if my replies are any indication. Mr. Fain goes on to another thought, which deserves especial consideration, since it says in so many words what many other executives have implied: "In the past decade or so, the art of business administration as an art or pseudo-science has been developed with text books, schools, etc., to a point where it is approached with the attitude that problems can be solved pretty much in the same manner that one solves a problem of bookkeeping, or of production; that is empirically. In foreign trade, however, I believe that the solving of problems, the determination of policies, must rely more upon good judgment than upon resort to rules and principles of administration."

No set of rules or principles of administration which can be offered in any business administration course will suffice to meet the varied problems and the frequent unknowns of business, domestic or foreign. Economic cycles, production, distribution and consumer demand are all at the mercy, in one way or another, of the fluctuations, variations and unknowns inherent in people. To rely on reasoned judgments based on a recognition of the human factor is the only way to meet the human problem present in all business relations. This controlling factor, the nature of the human being, cannot be isolated in any scientific absolute, or rendered clear in a working principle of business procedure, or limited to any quantitative or statistical estimate, or average. Such principles exist only in the sense of the existence of the average man. On the other hand, the fundamental recognition of the uniqueness of each individual leads to a relative approach which requires knowledge, clear reasoning power, judgment, and human, sympathetic understanding, in dealing with the individual. The humanities cultivate the mind in precisely these areas of mental development.

As Joseph C. Rovensky, prominent in the field of international banking, puts it: "One never knows enough. There is a great danger in knowing too little and even after one knows a lot on a subject, only then he realizes the complexity of things and has difficulty in arriving at conclusions. But, basically, world troubles are caused by selfishness, inequality of resources and of opportunities to go ahead, differences in humanities that populate the world, lack of knowledge of each other and everything that goes into human relations. Therefore, I cannot see how any one would question the necessity of a Liberal Arts education in general and foreign language studies in particular." If, as Mr. Rovensky implies, a relation exists between liberal arts education, and foreign language studies and an understanding of world troubles, here is a significant argument for the use of liberal studies to train business representatives of this nation for a better understanding of the role of this nation and of American business in the world community.

Still in a philosophical vein, Mr. Rovensky develops the idea that one never knows enough: "I spent my business life in foreign trade and finance. I traveled extensively, I knew many people—I still do— and I appreciate that no one will ever acquire an over-plus of schooling or training. This is the main thing that I think fellows like you have got to stress time and time again to the younger generation which comes to you at the beginning of its life's activities. . . . If you make him understand this without frightening him—make him realize what a fascinating and useful life he can have if he properly prepares himself—you will do a good job. And you must also tell him that the time spent in preparing himself is far from lost and that he will never attain a full life unless he is able to draw from the stores of the knowledge that he has gained of the Arts and Sciences, the activities of his fellow men all over the world in the past, the present—in order to look into the future."

Helen Mary Harding, Export Manager of the Doall Company, which has representatives in 56 countries, is in good position to speak for her sex in this presentation of executive opinion: "I hold from associations that liberal arts training is the best preparation for professional work, as well as for business and industry. I should qualify this by referring to 'long range preparation,' or liberal arts as a foundation for further specialized study. . . . Quite apart from the wider appreciation of the cultural values in life that liberal arts offered, I found that education of a general nature provided a good foundation for intensive or more specialized study. . . . The humanities course offers not only the background for advancing into specialized study, but in itself offers the best appreciation and undertaking for any kind of work or manner of living that one may do. . . . From my own limited experience in business, I consider it unfortunate that so many persons are so thoroughly 'skilled,' yet lack the general learning which provides an appreciation or imagination for something outside of one's own immediate job. The liberal arts course should, and in general does, strive at a more rounded or complete character and personality development, which thus makes possible the more efficient undertaking of any kind of work, whether it is highly professional or of a completely executive nature. While I can recall only a few remnants of Latin, I think 'quae sursum volo videre' reflects something of the spirit of liberal arts training."

The final paragraph of this letter contains a note of regret often sounded in the letters of reply: "Although there were very few actual courses I ever took in college that had any direct preparation for my present work, I consider that the liberal arts training offers the best background to enable one to do further study in the specific skills or training required. I never have regretted the four years spent in liberal arts preparation; I have often regretted that I neglected so flagrantly the opportunities for intensive study in the humanities and foreign languages that those four years offered."

The preceding quotations do no more than scratch the surface of the extensive body of information compiled under the heading of business and the liberal arts. I cannot resist offering two more samples of this material before turning to other matters. Austin S. Igleheart,

President of the General Foods Corporation, writes: "There is no question but that a liberal education is of assistance in all walks of life, particularly if it is effective in developing the ability to analyze and the ability to think, as well as to do both of these with an orderly mind." Howard Chase, Director of Public Relations, General Foods Corporation, offers the following analysis which supports the attitude suggested by Mr. Igleheart: "I attach extreme importance to liberal arts subjects as a background for success in business. With the world in flux for generations to come, men in business or in any other field of endeavor need the sense of awareness to human motivation which only a broad exposure to the humanities can give them. Success in business will always to a large degree depend on mastery of business techniques. In my opinion, however, never again will techniques be relatively as important to the successful production of goods and services as an understanding of the people who use those goods and services. . . . Over the long haul, however, the sense of direction upon which any institution will stand or fall will probably best come from men and women with broad interests in their own nation and in others."

In summary, the liberal arts—the humanities, together with a liberal introduction to the sciences—are presented as the best basic studies for success in any field of endeavor. Certainly it must be assumed that the individual possesses natural qualities of mind, heart and character, in order to profit most from these formal educational disciplines. In other words, a high quality of intelligence, a good character and high integrity are the best materials in the making of the individual of ability. The dominant trend of the letters of reply supports a conception of education which grants that certain kinds of education are superior in value and effectiveness to others, that the content of certain courses is of greater value to the development of the individual than the content of others. The liberal arts are presented as the kind of education most useful and most valuable to potential leaders in most spheres of activity.

In the beginning of this chapter, reference was made to the claims, most often voiced by professors of the liberal arts, that the humanities afford the best training of the mind, and therefore of the individual, for the higher intellectual tasks. Close consideration of the answers of business men reveals not only agreement with such a contention but even stronger support for the type of training afforded by the humanities.

VI

IMPLICATIONS AND CONCLUSIONS

THE IMMEDIATE PURPOSE of this investigation was to determine the views of business men, industrialists and governmental executives concerning the value of liberal arts training in general and languages in particular—including English—and to analyze these views, especially as part of a preparation for employment in business, industry and government. Accordingly, the opinions of an important and representative segment of American management regarding these subjects were collected, presented in summary, and commented upon. It is appropriate now to consider the material as a whole in seeking the implications and conclusions to be drawn from it.

That business executives consider liberal arts subjects of great importance has been reiterated throughout the course of this study. By far the most valuable of such subjects, as conducive to success in employment, is English. The ability to read, write, speak and understand English with the greatest possible facility, clarity and effectiveness, has been shown to be, in the opinion of reporting executives, the most essential of all the skills which any study of the humanities can impart.

Modern foreign languages are given a place second only to English among the liberal arts subjects. The cultural value of language study, the large contribution of language study to the development of essential general skills, such as the ability to understand, judge, discern, and think creatively, and the fundamental need of language skills for the successful pursuit of a wide variety of vocations, justify a far more important place for foreign language study in all curricula, from the late primary grades through high school and college. Furthermore, special emphasis is placed upon the need for more time to be spent in the study of foreign languages, so that an adequate facility may be acquired in all skills. Overemphasis upon one skill is not favored, since all are needed. In spite of the recognized value of oral skills, the ability to read a foreign language with full and accurate understanding is most frequently reported as the most important skill for obtaining employment. Foreign languages qualify under the heading of the humanities as the best preparation for the best jobs not because of any oral skill which may be acquired, but because of what they do to, and for, the individual through exercise of the mind, by deepening and broadening of the intellectual aspect of the human being. It is the conviction of many professors of language and literature and of many leading thinkers in the business world that this liberating influence justifies a central position for foreign language study in liberal arts curricula.

The implications of all the replies and other materials received during the course of this investigation touch many fields of thought and action. To be sure, the effect of the whole upon the intimate observer may not be quite the same as the immediate reaction aroused by the various parts. Therefore, my reaction to the whole may not coincide with that of even the individual contributors of the parts. For example, the individual contributors are not in a position to sense the development of a trend in the attitudes and thoughts expressed in all the letters. It is now my purpose to make as precise as I can at least some of the trends and currents of thought inherent in the response to my questions. The observations of the following pages are my own, and are not to be ascribed to any other person.

One of the most significant trends of executive opinion is that which favors liberal arts preparation over vocational skills as the best basic preparation for employment in business, industry and government. No distinction was drawn between superior students and average students or between positions at high levels or at low levels of responsibility, except possibly that the superior student would profit more than the average student, and that the liberal arts are more important as qualifications for positions of greater responsibility than for those which involve little or no executive responsibility. Speed in typing, the ability to operate office machines, and a knowledge of the mechanics of office procedure are, of course, valuable, but provide no substitute for a broad general education. Students who may seek employment above the level of manual labor need a kind of education which vocational training alone does not and cannot supply. Therefore, contrary to the belief of many high school and college students, the narrow vocational training for which they ask—and too often receive—is not proper or adequate training for the jobs which they will later seek.

The idea has been widely circulated in many quarters that since many students leave school too early, the substitution of vocational courses for such required courses as, for example, foreign languages will entice the students to remain in school longer. Another reason urged for such substitution is that vocational terminal course work is more practical and will better suit their needs in their future life work. Unfortunately, however, such a plan has the effect not only of reducing the value of the education for the superior student but also of not attaining the goal sought for the average student. The requirements which colleges are asked to relax—language, mathematics, etc.— are precisely those which will give even the average student what he needs most and will find most practical in his search for almost any job. Such a plan fails to serve the purposes and needs of students and employers alike.

To clarify the distinction between a liberal arts education and a vocational training, a few words of explanation are offered here.

Studies in the liberal arts in general, and in the humanities in particular, are concerned with the development of *basic,* or *general skills,* just as vocational training is concerned with the development of *specific skills* involving techniques, or how something is done. When using the term "general skills" in the course of this report, I had in mind the ability to learn, the ability to recognize problems in their true light and to attack them in a clear, logical, even imaginative way, with full awareness of their broadest context and their specific significance, the ability to think well and to express thoughts clearly and concisely. These abilities, which were so often mentioned in letters from executives as belonging to the person with a liberal education, are the result of a cultivation of the mind in the development of its more general abilities, rather than in the training of the fragmentary but often unrelated skills of the individual. The ideal here is the formation of an individual who, in spite of the general nature of his education, is able to use his knowledge as a base for the solution of the many varying problems with which he will be faced.

Although the whole weight of the information compiled in the course of this investigation favors the kind of education which develops best and most surely these general skills—a liberal education— full attention was given vocational skills as well. Employment in business and industry requires vocational skills, since secretaries must be proficient in taking dictation and in typing, salesmen must know how to sell, engineers must know the technical aspects of their profession, and executives must possess managerial skills. The point is that these vocational skills, or any others, need to be offered in combination with the general skills and the general knowledge obtained from studies in the humanities. An attempt to specialize in vocational subjects at the high school level results in exclusion of the minimum of general knowledge and skills which can successfully support vocational competence. The exclusion of humanities from college-level studies in favor of specialized vocational training results in a one-sided competence which places a ceiling on the usefulness of the person to business employers, and which creates a barrier to advancement and higher salaries that only years of study and work can overcome. It would seem to be unfair to students at any level to deny them, by an over-emphasis upon vocational training, the essentials of an education which will prepare them better for life, as well as for making a living. Adjustment to life is not to be had from fragmentary and specific competencies, but from a strong, capable, flexible mind developed and enriched through contact with the humanities. Since language is essential in the development of the mind through familiarity with the best of thought in this and other ages, the study of languages occupies a key position in the educational process.

After reading those letters which describe in detail the kind of education and training which employers want their employees to have, I have come to the conclusion that the American educational system is falling far short of satisfying the minimum needs of business and industry. Since business is the largest employer of the graduates of our schools, and since those persons who look to business as their source of livelihood make up a very large part of this nation, I must conclude that the American educational system—the secondary school system in particular—does not adequately serve the needs of this nation. To be sure, educators may point to crowded conditions in the schools, shortages of teachers, lack of physical facilities, and the insufficient supply of the more recently developed aids to teaching. Important as these obstacles to good teaching may be, they do not touch the root of the problem. The fault seems to lie in an unbalanced curriculum, in a failure to insist upon the ability to read, write and speak our own language and that of others, in a failure to stress throughout the educational system the essential intellectual nature of education, in the downgrading of higher education to a level which approaches mediocrity, and in a general laxness and lack of discipline, particularly of the mind, which bids fair to lower the level of our national intellectual competence.

That business, industry and government urgently need well qualified personnel is revealed by the tone and content of the letters which I have received. While leadership at every level is becoming increasingly important, we fail to train the leaders needed. Since the number of qualified personnel and the number of persons qualified for leadership, particularly for service at the management level is decidedly inadequate, the implications are clear. The work of the American schools must be lifted above the level of that which may be acquired with ease by average, or even below average students, to a level which offers a real challenge to the average students, and even to superior students. The reason is simple enough: the strength and survival of business, industry and government rest heavily on the best brains and the finest abilities which this nation can produce. It follows that a public school system which permits its best student minds to fall into a state of intellectual laziness and disuse does not serve even the best interests of those persons of more modest ability whose interests are often assumed to be the first and chief responsibility of the school system. Important also is the fact that it is unfair for business to have to offer training on company time and at company expense, often under the heading of orientation programs, which should have been done in the schools.

Within the scope of the opinion surveyed in this report, liberal arts and the humanities have been shown to be of key importance in the development of the individual, of society, and of understanding at the international level. Persons in high places in both business and in government recognize the need of supporting adequately nontechnical education and research. Yet the major proportion of funds from both government and industry are available only for "practical" research. At the beginning of this past year, only three per cent of the total of funds allotted for research by government and industry was assigned to the humanities, the social studies, and the liberal arts. Fully ninety-seven per cent of the total funds available were assigned to what is called applied research.[1] This shocking disproportion undoubtedly continues. Those business and governmental leaders who believe in the value of the humanities need to look more closely at the distribution of those funds which they earmark for specific projects. After all, with the increased prestige of the "human

[1] Benjamin Fine, in "Education in Review," *The New York Times,* December 11, 1949, offers the following breakdown: "engineering sciences, 37 per cent; physical sciences, 25 per cent; biological sciences, 21 per cent, and agricultural sciences, 14 per cent. Only 3 per cent is left for the humanities, the social studies or the liberal arts."

relations" approach in labor-management relations and in society in general, the human side, as represented by the humanities and social studies, deserves far better support than it is getting. An overemphasis upon technical and scientific development can be justified only briefly and partly because of war conditions, since the nature, quality, attitude and skill of the people who must use the benefits of modern technical development are obviously more important than the technical developments themselves. When real peace does come to the world, research done in the humanities may well assume a role which will be more important than that which is now played by scientific and technical research.

In conclusion, the vital contribution that the humanities should make to the society of our time should not be stifled by an educational philosophy which decries the development of the mind to its highest level of achievement. A new and stronger emphasis on the humanities must replace the present trend toward de-emphasis if we are to attain our most cherished goals, for only by striving to develop our minds to the fullest possible degree can we make real progress.

APPENDICES

I

EMPLOYMENT IN BUSINESS
AND INDUSTRY

MANY ATTRACTIVE POSITIONS are available to persons who have foreign language skills as well as competence in technical, commercial or managerial aspects of business. There are also a number of profitable uses to which a specialized knowledge of foreign languages may be put. The purpose of this section is to present some of the details concerning the fields of employment in which the greatest demand for persons trained in languages has been reported, the qualifications for the positions most frequently described, salary ranges, and other pertinent facts related to opportunities for employment. All the available material on this subject cannot be released, since much of it was sent solely for the purpose of determining the general conclusions of the survey. Therefore, within the framework of the above restriction, I shall consider the most frequently mentioned and most valuable kinds of vocational opportunities for persons offering adequate training in foreign languages.

MANAGEMENT

Management, as a field of opportunity for language-trained personnel, received special attention in the letters received from contributing executives. These men have daily need of broad general knowledge, creative imagination, flexibility of viewpoint in adjustments to ever-changing conditions, sharp perception where variables of human conduct touch economic life, understanding of what goes on in the minds of other people throughout the world, and language skills which assure clear, forceful communication.

I am led to believe that the person who studies a foreign language with the direct intention of becoming a translator, an interpreter, or a teacher, is not necessarily the type who will receive favorable consideration for a position in management. According to replies from some of my inquiries the person who gives an important place to foreign language study in a liberal arts education as a cultural and mind-developing experience has a good chance of being favorably considered, if that person also includes courses essential in business preparation, such as mathematics, accounting, economics, and perhaps some business administration courses. Above the level of the general education represented by the A. B., even a minimum amount of specialized training in business, financial and technical subjects, centered about the products of the business in which employment is sought, will go a long way toward assuring employment.

In all fairness to those who place their faith in the vocational value of skill in speaking and writing a foreign language, it must be said that such skills can play a large part in securing positions in management in a number of business enterprises. This is true because American business in general has assumed international characteristics, and is becoming more international in character each day. Few firms of any size can escape foreign contacts, either through import or export. Even companies which serve the domestic market must commonly seek raw materials abroad, or study the possibility of competition from foreign producers. More and more, even these companies are surveying the foreign market with a view to expansion. Here is a large and growing field of opportunity for those who add competence in foreign languages to other qualifications.

Large companies are often unable to find sufficient fully qualified executives. Higher management is actively seeking promising young people whom they can train for the essential work at the higher executive levels. Only certain types are suitable to the work, but even those who qualify through intelligence and personal characteristics may find the doors of opportunity closed to them because of such weaknesses as lack of facility in English and lack of general culture. Although a future executive may still have to start at the bottom, the day of the Horatio Alger conception of moving up the executive ladder by hard work and experience alone seems to be coming to an end. The very nature of modern business requires special training never before required. More and more it can be said that education—enough of it, and the right kind—"pays off."

Employers are placing increased emphasis upon advanced degrees for persons with commercial or technical training. This trend reflects either dissatisfaction with what is achieved at the undergraduate level, or additional demands upon such persons brought about by the increasing complexity of science and business.

Requirements are high for better positions, but so are the salaries. Most of the executive positions brought to my attention in this investigation fall within the range of $10,000 to $25,000 per year. Seldom were they lower than $6,000, and in a few cases salaries above $25,000 per year were suggested. Any ambitious person with intelligence and favorable personal characteristics who seeks a field of employment in which the challenge is great and the satisfactions many will do well to study the needs and requirements of American management.

The greatest value of the remarks on preparation for positions in management, lies in the widespread recognition reported, particularly at the highest levels of management, of the practical value of general skills and knowledge which are nurtured and developed in the course of a liberal education. And it goes without saying that foreign languages occupy an important place in the liberal arts curriculum.

FOREIGN TRADE

Foreign Trade is the largest and the most obvious area of opportunity for persons who possess foreign language skills. The breadth of the field today, its infinite variety, and its tremendous potential growth may escape the notice of both the student and the curriculum planner. In spite of the strong demand for specialized personnel, there is a serious shortage of courses and curriculum plans leading to the right kind of preparation for service in our expanding foreign trade.

Since business and industrial operations abroad are already so far developed, the range of positions available abroad is quite as wide as that of positions in this country. Yet qualifications which suffice for employment in this country do not necessarily equip a person for service in foreign posts. Truly effective service in foreign areas requires knowledge and skills which are not always listed among the requirements for work in the home office. Among these are foreign language skills, knowledge of the cultural products of foreign areas, and understanding of foreign economic problems and practices. A knowledge of religious and political influences, attitudes of the people toward other nations, economic and market potentials, and the aspirations of the people is also extremely useful. Such broad preparation is all too often lacking among persons otherwise qualified for technical and commercial positions. It is only natural that business firms have had to turn to natives in their search for qualified persons to fill important technical and executive positions not covered by local restrictive laws on the hiring of non-nationals. No matter how satisfactory the service of these nationals may be, many executives express the opinion that their firm would much prefer to place Americans in these positions. But they are frequently not to be had, since so few persons in this country are adequately prepared in the right combination of language, area, business, and technical subjects.

A. R. Lillicrapp, Treasurer and Export Manager of the Dixie Cup Company, expresses faith in the important role played by international trade in the economic life of this country: "It is my firm conviction that international trade is going to be—if it is not already—pretty much the salvation of this country and certainly to other countries throughout the world. No country on earth can exist without its foreign trade. . . . As far as this country is concerned, it is not to be supposed that we can paddle our own canoe exclusively, sell our merchandise to other countries and do little or no buying from them." This quotation is typical of the views expressed in a great many letters.

Since hundreds of thousands of persons are required to carry on trade with foreign areas, and since large numbers of these persons need some specialized training in foreign languages, an estimate of the demand for language trained personnel could be set at a figure which would indicate that foreign trade is a rich field of employment for those who will seek the proper preparation for it. Many persons now serving in commercial or technical capacities in this country, as well as abroad, have daily need of special preparation which they did not bring to their present jobs. These employees are being urged, and sometimes required, to fill such gaps by study after business hours, or by attending courses offered by the company at company expense and on company time. This awakening of employers to the need of their employees for such courses as foreign languages and studies of foreign areas can only mean that persons employed in these jobs in the future must offer such training as part of their qualifications. War conditions will not alter the fact that persons offering such training are and will be needed; such personnel will be sought after by governmental agencies just as they are by business and industry.

To give a rough sketch of vocational opportunities in foreign trade, it will be necessary to mention only four major divisions. First, there are the multi-million-dollar corporations whose volume of business justifies the formation of international divisions as subsidiary corporations. Second, there are the companies whose volume of business with foreign areas justifies an export department. Third, there are export firms, large and small, which specialize in serving companies which do not set up their own export organization. Fourth, there are firms which specialize in foreign trade services, such as forwarding, packaging, insurance, and other matters essential in foreign trade. It is essential to stress at this point that when the term "export" is used here, import is also implied in most cases, since foreign trade is a two-way proposition. Thousands of firms which do not stress export must import various materials for the manufacture of goods for sale in this country.

If I am to believe the letters received from executives in the major international divisions of American corporations, these international companies have been overestimated as a source of opportunities for persons trained in foreign languages. It seems that the largest number of such opportunities will be found in the sum total of the demand for such personnel in the very large number of smaller companies. On the other hand, I am led to believe that the opportunities for employment in international companies deserve special attention because of the size, power, and potential expansion of such units.

Alex J. Wertis, Personnel Manager, United States Steel Export Company, enclosed with his letter a copy of his article, "So You Want An Overseas Assignment," a digest of which appeared in *The Management Review* (June, 1948). In this article, Mr. Wertis writes, under the heading of "Languages": "The ability to speak or to learn a foreign language is a tremendous asset. The greatest criticism of Americans in foreign lands in the past has been their reluctance to meet other peoples half-way about languages. Other peoples take as much pride in their language and culture as we do in ours. To address them in their own speech is a compliment to their language and culture. It gives you a head start in personal relations." Under the heading of "Professional Requirements," Mr. Wertis includes a thorough reading and speaking knowledge of at least one foreign language of commercial importance. In his discussion of the need for adequately trained personnel at various levels of service, Mr. Wertis mentions the following: clerical positions; supervisory, technical and non-technical positions; line and staff positions within the general office; and overseas assignment in various capacities.

Some elements of the general pattern of all the letters received may be detected in this information sent by Mr. Wertis. First of all, the great importance of the role of training in foreign languages in foreign trade work is recognized. Next, the quality of the individual is given appropriate emphasis as the key factor in his success. The ability to do clear, level-headed thinking supersedes other abilities, whether specific or general. In the opinion of reporting executives, it is at this level that the liberal education to be had through contact with the humanities can make its greatest contribution. The range of the positions mentioned by Mr. Wertis—which includes both clerk and top executive—is in complete harmony with the spread of opportunity in foreign trade indicated by the pattern of all the letters received from executives in foreign trade.

Elijah G. Poxson, General Staff, General Motors Overseas Operations, agrees with Mr. Wertis in stressing certain natural qualities of the man and his ability to do the specific job, over the ability to speak a foreign language. Mr. Poxson writes: "In our Overseas Operations, vocational opportunity is not predicated on language ability, but rather upon a man's fitness for the opening. Naturally his fitness presupposes his capacity to acquire the proper working knowledge of the language in the country to which he may be sent." On the other hand, Mr. Poxson goes on to say: "It is always extremely helpful and advantageous if a person being assigned to a country has a previous knowledge of that country."

Some firms have relied in the past on promises of employees that they will learn the language of the country to which they are to be sent after they arrive in the area. Such promises and expectations have not always yielded satisfactory results. In fact, it is becoming increasingly necessary for employers to insist that employees acquire a knowledge of foreign languages before assignment to the field. The statement of C. W. Linscheid, Manager of the Export Division of Fairbanks Morse and Company, Inc., is typical: "We are insisting now that applicants have a definite knowledge of the language that will be required before they are employed as our experience has been that a promise to study and acquire proficiency in a language after employment is seldom achieved."

At the executive level, some companies foresee the need of requiring a certain number of those in management to be trained in foreign languages. Speaking of long-term plans, J. F. McCrudden, Export Manager of the Aberfoyle Manufacturing Company says: "In visualizing the development of the Aberfoyle Manufacturing Company during the next quarter of a century, we believe that there will be established a requirement for a given number of the executive branch of its organization to be trained in foreign languages." Some foreign traders take the position that only those who are fully and adequately prepared in foreign languages are truly equipped to engage in foreign trade, whether such persons belong to the executive branch or not. G. G. Cobean, President of the Bulkley, Dunton Paper Company, which has sales offices in forty-two cities in Latin America, Europe, the Near East, the Far East, and the Union of South Africa, is one of those who take this view: "Permit me to say that any young persons who intend to engage in foreign business are really not equipped to do so unless they *speak fluently* at least such a language as Spanish or French. Portuguese is also a necessary language if one intends to engage in business in Brazil. . . . When I say that a knowledge of the language is necessary, I mean a really fluent and complete understanding of the language, and not the pidgin variety with which most graduates from our high schools, and even our colleges, are turned out in this country." Mr. Cobean goes on to offer reasons for the importance of an adequate knowledge of a foreign language: "Anyone attempting to do business with people in foreign countries who cannot speak to them in their own language in such a manner as to make it easy for the foreigner to converse with them, is in exactly the same condition as a boxer who enters the rings with one arm tied behind him. My lifetime of experience in foreign countries and in foreign business has taught me that anyone who must depend upon a third person to translate his thoughts and proposals is most severely handicapped, as it is not possible for him to win the personal friendship of the foreign customer, and that is the most important factor to take into consideration in doing business with foreign people."

Among the executives in world trade who consider proper language training a primary qualification for those who would serve well, either at home or abroad, is R. Vizcarrondo, Foreign Sales Manager, The Baldwin Piano Company. Since he offers a statement so representative of this group, I quote his letter in some detail:

"In my 35 years of exporting I have found that foreign languages are not a secondary but a primary qualification in exporting, for the following reasons:

"1) A person intending to follow an exporting or importing career has to start at the foot of the ladder as an office assistant, stenographer or some other clerical position, if he or she aspires to a position where he or she can direct and teach subalterns. With a knowledge of foreign languages such a person is more valuable in the export or import department of any firm and can demand more salary than one without this qualification.

"2) A person trained in foreign languages, especially a man, has a much better opportunity to become a traveling representative, either as a salesman in the export business or a buyer in the import business, than one without such qualifications, and he not only can demand a better remuneration than a similar employee in the domestic field, but can also have an opportunity to see the world without costing him anything.

"3) With a knowledge of foreign languages such a representative can do a much better job for his employers, for he can read the local newspapers and know what is happening in each country and converse with his business connections in their own language, not merely from the American point of view but from their point of view as well.

"4) To prove the value of personnel trained in foreign languages, whenever I have to use the services of an outside translator for foreign languages that we do not write in this Department, we have to pay from $4.00 to $5.00 for the average one-page letter, which a good translator can write in from 15 to 20 minutes, if it is not a technical letter, but just a regular commercial letter.

"5) Even though the distributors or customers of an exporting firm may write English, they need catalogues and other publicity material in the language of the country where they may be selling the goods, and if the exporting firm has to send such material out to be translated, it not only is very expensive but usually it is poorly translated because outside translators generally are not familiar with the construction of the goods covered by the translation, and they cannot describe the specifications of the goods in an understandable language if they are not familiar with their construction. Being a linguist myself and having done a lot of translating in the past, I know whereof I speak.

"6) A person trained in foreign languages also has many opportunities to secure a position in foreign countries at a higher salary than he or she would get in this country in similar work, with one of the many American companies operating abroad, and thus have an opportunity to perfect himself or herself in foreign languages and see the world.

"I do not claim that a knowledge of foreign languages is the only qualification for success in foreign trade, but it is an uppermost help in getting into it and making a success of it."

Whether the position sought in international trade is technical, clerical or executive in nature, the person adequately trained in foreign languages is at a distinct advantage. The statement of Joseph S. Goldware, International Sales Department, Blue Star Foods, Inc., bears this out: "Nearly all the positions in foreign trade from the lowest salary group to the highest are enhanced by foreign language ability. In other words, what we are trying to say is that along with the basic knowledge of a foreign language must come the same sort of specific training which anybody engaging in commercial trade in the United States must have. This goes for stenographers, salesmen, executives, foreign freight forwarders, advertising men, etc."

The preceding quotation demonstrates a basic assumption of this survey. A person with stenographic skills may get a job as a stenographer. But, the stenographer with adequately developed language skills may not only qualify as a bilingual stenographer, but may be considered for more attractive positions in foreign trade or in domestic business.

Foreign representatives of business houses must offer more than foreign languages, competence in technical details, and experience: certain personal qualities are also essential. H. Lyman Smith, Director of the Foreign Trade Bureau, St. Louis Chamber of Commerce, mentions intellectual curiosity as a primary requisite for persons who would be valuable to a foreign trade department. He goes on to say: "Another thing that is important in an exporter is his attitude toward difficulty. There are over 90 different areas in which foreign trade is being done. Each one has its own regulations which are changed, some almost daily. Restrictions are constantly being placed in the way of the exporter. If he accepts these as barring him from the market he belongs in some other type of business. A resourceful exporter finds perfectly legal means of getting his goods into a country where other exporters have not tried hard enough."

It goes without saying that the person who can follow Mr. Smith's advice needs to know not only the English and the American economic scene, but needs also a thorough and dependable knowledge of the economic, legal, linguistic, psychological and cultural aspects which control the situation in the foreign area. For example, some American advertising and selling practices which are effective here may not only be offensive abroad, but may actually be prohibited by law. Often a psychological barrier concerning the color of the package, or the nature of the language or the illustrations used in advertising, or even the excessive use of otherwise psychologically correct advertising may prevent the sale of goods abroad. In one area, only high quality will sell the merchandise; in another area, low cost will be enough to effect a sale. One will not find a list of all such problems, with workable solutions, between the covers of any book. Neither will experience alone provide the understanding necessary to any successful attempt to penetrate a foreign market. Clearly, the ambitious foreign trader does need intellectual curiosity, tenacity and resourcefulness, as Mr. Smith suggests. But in order to make these qualities effective, the foreign trader—even the beginner who starts at the bottom—must have special training and experience. Too many persons have relied on advice which discounts the value of studies in the language, literature, and history of foreign lands. In addition to qualifications based on engineering, commercial or executive skills, a thorough grounding in liberal studies, with special attention to foreign languages and cultural studies seems to constitute the minimum educational preparation for the person who wishes to advance in the foreign trade field.

Language training is necessary in all branches of foreign trade, including sales, engineering, and distribution. Roger R. Dulong, Export Sales Manager of the Carter Carburetor Corporation speaks for his firm as follows: "It is absolutely necessary that a representative of this company who is sent out into the field anywhere in the world, have a thorough knowledge of at least one language other than English, whether he be in work dealing with sales, engineering, or distribution. We believe that there is no effective substitute for knowing and speaking the other person's language, either for brevity, clarity, or courtesy."

Because of the increased number of business men in foreign areas who speak English and who write their business letters in English, some American exporters feel that they can rely on English to carry on their business. On the other hand, the majority of the foreign trade executives who answered my questions feel that business is more effectively and efficiently transacted in the language of the foreign buyer or seller than it is in English. Furthermore, some firms cannot count on finding a situation abroad which favors the use of English. Such a possibility is mentioned in the following remarks by William L. Neilson, Jr., Export Manager of the Greenfield Tap and Die Corporation: "As far as language is concerned the Export Manager or export salesman is in a position to do a much better job in those countries in which he can speak the language. Again, the fact that this company is engaged in selling mechanic's tools means that the buyers are for the most part hardware stores owned and operated by nationals who speak only their own language. The contact and exchange of ideas between the importer and the salesman are weakened and even destroyed when the conversation must be carried on through a third party."

Although Mr. Neilson and a few others find that the business conversation abroad seldom rises above the purely material points related to the proposed purchase or sale, many other foreign traders report that the direct, high-pressure salesmanship often characteristic of the American approach at some levels alienates overseas buyers. It is often necessary to use an indirect approach, and to meet the foreign buyer on a cultural level. The point is that many courses now considered educational luxuries for the prospective foreign trader are really necessities.

Roger R. Dulong, whose letter was cited above, states a very practical reason for the general study of foreign peoples and areas: "We feel that intensive study of the conditions, people, habits, and general information of a country is essential." More specialized studies, of the sort most often suggested throughout this investigation as belonging to the post-graduate level, are stressed in Mr. Dulong's next statement: "In our particular work, we must insist upon a knowledge of our product from both an engineering and a selling standpoint. And, of course, the experience in all manufacturing and industrial courses combined with studies of marketing, retailing, and general business practices, is necessary." The combination of language training and technical training has often been preferred by reporting executives to a combination of language training and commercial studies, for the reason that opportunities for employment are greater for the first combination. Although few candidates for employment offer ideal combinations of knowledge and ability, those who do will be appropriately rewarded.

Henry J. Ebert, Manager of the Export Division of the Cleaver-Brooks Company, is pessimistic about the need for foreign language skills in the export field. Yet he presents the following ideal combination: "From a standpoint of a manufacturer of engineering equipment, the ideal combination would be a man with knowledge of foreign languages, a mechanical or electrical engineer as the case may be, and primarily a seasoned foreign trader; but unfortunately there are not many men in this country of these qualifications, and those who have these qualifications can command a premium because they have spent years, the hard way, to come up through the mill."

New posts are being created in a number of companies which feel the need for persons who can serve in the fields of foreign market analysis and sales promotion in foreign areas. It is essential that more Americans be trained well enough to qualify for such positions.

For those who like certain aspects of foreign trade work, but who do not care to go abroad, a statement by W. G. LaPoe, Assistant Employment Manager, General Personnel Department, The Armstrong Cork Company, is of special interest. Attention is called to the fact that two organizations within this company are directly concerned with either production, or distribution, abroad. The Export Division sells abroad all products produced in the nineteen domestic plants throughout the United States, as well as the products manufactured in the foreign plants. The Foreign Operations Department is responsible for the operation of the foreign plants located in Canada, England, Spain, Portugal, North Africa and the Union of South Africa. Against this broad background, Mr. LaPoe reports:

"We employ a number of linguistic secretaries in our Export Division at the home office, who have the responsibility of translating letters from abroad into English and translating English dictation into the language of the country to which the correspondence is being sent.

"We require the knowledge of Spanish, French and/or Portuguese on the part of our men to be trained as salesmen for foreign assignment. In the case of an individual to be assigned to one of our foreign plants in an operating capacity, i.e., accountant, engineer, etc., the knowledge of a foreign language is not as important as in the case of the salesman; however, we prefer the individual to have some basic background in language study.

"With regard to the linguistic secretaries, they must be proficient in secretarial work, i.e., shorthand, typing, etc. In the case of a foreign salesman, he must be a graduate from a four-year college course having majored in business administration, economics, liberal arts, or some form of engineering.

"For an accountant's assignment—an accounting major in college; and an engineering degree for an engineer assigned to one of our foreign plants.

"We feel that it is highly desirable that information concerning the economics, practices, customs and attitudes of the areas where the language is spoken be presented in combination with a language course."

The following excerpt from a letter from A. R. Hauschel, Vice President of the J. I. Case Company, may sound like bad news to the student just out of college, but it should sound most heartening to those mature persons who have already gained knowledge and experience in the field of the manufacture and sale of machinery: "A knowledge of foreign languages, and particularly Spanish, French and

Portuguese, is deemed necessary in our foreign work in certain territories. A still more important prerequisite is a thorough knowledge of our product, and since we manufacture over one hundred different types of machinery we follow the practice of not sending any men abroad until they have had at least a few years experience with us in the United States so as to become more fully familiar with the merits of our product and our ways of doing business. Furthermore, for such positions we prefer to send men of more mature age (not younger than 30) instead of men just out of college, who generally lack business experience and therefore could hardly cope with the various problems they would have to meet in their tasks."

The implications of this quotation are important, since there are undoubtedly many men of some experience with manufactured products who, with additional training in night school, or home study in foreign languages and other recommended studies, might become eligible for foreign assignment at much higher salaries. This information is directed as much to persons already serving in business as it is to college and high school students who seek to prepare well for business careers. The breadth of the field of opportunity for those who seek the additional training needed to qualify for higher posts is made clear in the following remarks by J. vB. Dresser, Assistant Export Manager of Canada Dry International: "There is always a demand for American engineers and specialists who speak foreign languages—but today more and more men trained in sales and distribution are needed. American methods of advertising, selling and merchandising are being studied and copied abroad more each year. Men experienced in general export-import business are required in many industries. . . . As the world grows smaller and American business expands its contacts abroad there is every reason to expect more need for men trained in foreign languages."

Typical of the letters which express a desire to hire Americans instead of foreign nationals, when adequately prepared Americans are to be had, is that of L. J. Fletcher, Director of Training and Community Relations, The Caterpillar Tractor Company: "In a number of foreign countries we have, in the past, utilized both natives of the country whom we have given training here in the use of our product, as well as American technically trained men who have had some opportunity to learn the foreign language and customs. Among other things, we have learned that the residents of foreign countries, when considering the purchase of machinery equipment such as ours, place a great deal more confidence in a native American with experience here than they do in people of their own countries. This is because our work abroad consists largely of recommending certain types and sizes of machinery for certain jobs, most of which have not heretofore been accomplished by mechanical means. Investments are rather large, and the foreign investor wants to make certain that the job can be done according to the claims made by the seller. On the other hand, we have had some rather expensive experience with native born representatives whose enthusiasms for the performance of our product considerably exceeded their ability to translate job requirements into machines. You see, the language of success or failure of the machine on the job is universal. . . . It is true that there is considerable loss and additional expense when attempting to work through interpreters. In many situations, however, this is much preferred to lack of technical ability."

Roy S. Jones, Vice President, The Coca-Cola Export Sales Company, mentions the practice of his company, with reference to the hiring of Americans who offer a combination of technical skills and foreign language training. Here again, both qualifications are essential: "We sometimes find it necessary to employ Americans who have special skills to work in our business, such as chemical engineers, mechanical engineers, and accountants. People with these special qualifications, who are also well trained in the beverage industry, are desired from time to time for overseas assignment. It is, of course, necessary that such personnel speak fluently the language of the country in which they are to be assigned."

J. K. Jenney, Assistant Director, Foreign Relations Department, E. I. du Pont de Nemours and Company, stresses the importance of the addition of a liberal arts education, including language, to the technical courses for chemists and engineers who are interested in moving up to important managerial posts. In the du Pont organization, the necessary business or technical background is obviously the first consideration in choosing persons for work in foreign areas, as Mr. Jenney points out. Yet, in order to be successful, he says that these men "must have or acquire language qualifications and an understanding of the customs of the country to which they are assigned and the mentality of the people thereof." After speaking of the difficulty of securing all these qualifications in one man, Mr. Jenney goes on to say: "Obviously, if men have both sets of qualifications their opportunities for selection and advancement are much greater than others who only have the necessary vocational qualifications. . . .

Young men who can add to the requisite technical education a knowledge of languages, history, etc., are very much in demand for foreign job opportunities."

The salary range for foreign trade, as suggested by the employers themselves, is wide indeed. K. E. Deardorff, Office Manager, Export Department, Euclid Road Machinery Company, offers a typical general statement about salary: "Salaries, of course, are dependent to a great extent on the individual and the type of organization with which he is working. A number of companies have small export departments where their export manager is probably earning from seven to ten thousand dollars each year. In bigger companies, the salary is adjusted accordingly. There is a trend now toward companies forming a separate export company to handle all export transactions. In this case, the export manager becomes the president of the new company. To justify a separate company, the sales volume must be large and, of course, the salary of the individual at the head of the company is appropriate." Walter A. Vela, Export Manager of Graflex, Inc., reports the salary range in the following manner: "Foreign Field Representatives, Branch Managers and Export Executives move within salary ranges of $4,000 to $25,000 and up, this great gap existing because of different company policies, responsibilities, volume of business transactions, capabilities, etc." In short, the range reported includes positions at $30 per week for some secretarial jobs and much more than $25,000 in some high managerial posts. Most of the positions reported were executive in nature, so that salaries reported were quite commonly above $10,000. It goes without saying that the larger salaries are open only to persons of experience who offer the proper qualifications.

SALES

The field of Sales received very favorable mention in a great number of replies. Unfortunately, most of the information about sales positions appeared in restricted letters. Therefore I can only present a few brief remarks under this important heading.

Selling, both here and abroad, is the big job ahead of American business. At least this is the opinion of many American business men. Present markets offer a continuing and attractive field of opportunity for the effective salesman. Good jobs at practically every level are to be had for the person who offers the right combination of personal characteristics, knowledge of the product, educational and cultural background, and selling ability.

Letters from sales managers and executive officers of large companies are in agreement on the important contribution of a liberal education in the formation of an individual able to meet and understand customers at all levels. The successful salesman is aided in attaining mastery of the art of understanding the other person through language and its application in literature. Obviously, theory and practice need to be joined, so that liberal studies would be completed by practical application in experience.

In general the letters of reply discuss two areas of opportunity for sales personnel. They are the domestic sales operations of American business, and foreign sales operations. A liberal arts education, including foreign languages, was held to provide the best basic preparation for both kinds of employment.

In retail selling, particularly in industrial areas with high concentrations of foreign workers, and in urban areas where foreign buyers may appear frequently, the well prepared merchant needs to have someone available who can use the language of the foreign buyers. Large stores and hotels in large cities, particularly port centers, maintain special personnel chosen for their ability to serve the foreign customer in his own language. But the great opportunity in selling is at the wholesale level. The salesmen in the better paying posts in this division are the ones most likely to be chosen for elevation to important foreign assignments, after they have obtained a thorough knowledge of the business and the product. At this point foreign language skills and knowledge of foreign areas become key factors in the advancement and the effectiveness of the salesman who has begun his service in the domestic organization. According to information received, many salesmen in the domestic organization are chosen with a view to their possible transfer to the export or import division of the company, or to active work in foreign sales, market development, etc. In such cases, the possession of language skills is extremely valuable to the individual, and to the company.

In the higher management brackets, salaries are large, both in this country and abroad. A. A. Verner, Sales Manager of the Export Division of the Kelly-Springfield Tire Company says: "Generally speaking, the salary range in the lower categories will run approximately 25% higher than the average prevailing in this country and, in the top income brackets, they will be about the same."

Opportunities abroad for sales representatives are many and attractive. Their role is important and they are well paid. Since so many foreign representatives need to be, or must be, technically trained, the nature of the opportunities for the foreign technical representative serving in sales is essentially the same as the kind of opportunity already mentioned for technical personnel in foreign trade. Furthermore, since much of the selling abroad is done through, or in close relation to, the export division of the producing firm, or a firm specializing in foreign trade, the field of opportunity for sales personnel abroad will resemble, or may even be identical with that of foreign trade.

ENGINEERS AND OTHER TECHNICALLY TRAINED PERSONS

Engineers and other technically trained persons who include in their preparation adequate training in the liberal arts in general and in foreign languages in particular are especially favored by a large number of employers. The greatest demand in business and government seems to be for combinations of technical competence and ability in sales, knowledge of economic, historical and cultural aspects of foreign areas, experience in foreign trade, or managerial skills. However, since adequate preparation in such combinations of skills and knowledge cannot be acquired in a four-year technical course, or in a strictly liberal arts preparation, or in specialized studies in business administration or foreign trade, there are very few persons being trained today for such important and highly paid positions. Employers are being forced to accept inadequately trained personnel and to attempt to train these persons on company time and at company expense. The resulting delay in developing fully qualified personnel is serious and costly for the company. Employees who wish to rise to attractive positions of responsibility in their chosen field are unnecessarily delayed in their advancement for long periods of time.

A great many executives in engineering and other firms express the opinion that training and knowledge other than that involving experience with company procedure and the company's product can and should be acquired in school and college. But if adequate background in the liberal arts is to be had, technical and specialized training must be delayed at least until the junior year of college and in many cases until the post-graduate level of education. Thus, technical employers in a number of firms have expressed opinions which favor at least five and, more often, six years as the minimum training period for scientific and technical personnel. Until the preparation of students entering college is greatly improved, so that college teachers will not find it necessary to occupy themselves with details and subjects which belong to the work of the secondary schools, some of the college-level work must be postponed until the graduate level.

The engineer who offers language skills and a broader educational background than others of his calling is prepared for a wide variety of jobs and for a better salary in sales positions or in positions involving direct technical service abroad. The list of companies which need technical personnel trained in foreign languages is especially long, since it includes corporations operating here and abroad in every branch of manufacture, processing, construction, distribution, etc.

Many of the most desirable positions reported involve executive duties. Adequate executive material is hard to find, and executive positions command as a result premium salaries. One example of the financial opportunity in such positions is found in the letter of William M. Healy, Manager of the Export Sales Department of the Rheem Manufacturing Company:

"The Rheem Manufacturing Company has had considerable experience recently in operations outside the continental limits of the United States. One of our problems has been the obtaining of properly qualified personnel to fill executive positions in our overseas plants, overseas offices, and in conducting market surveys in the various markets in which we feel developments are of interest to us.

"It is our feeling that adequate knowledge of the language of the country in which this personnel is to be operating is extremely important. . . .

"We also send engineers who are engaged in supervising the construction of our plants and the actual management, and from time to time sales personnel.

"The salaries range from $800.00 to $1200.00 per month with expenses paid.

"The more they are grounded in the cultural background of the country in which they are to operate the greater their value."

It is evident that opportunities for technical personnel with foreign language and cultural background are many and attractive. Surely such a favorable field deserves more attention and more adequate preparation on the part of those who lean in the direction of science and technology.

ADVERTISING

Advertising, Newspaper Work, Public Relations and Radio have also received strong support as fields of employment for persons trained in foreign languages. Contrary to the pessimistic views of a few advertising executives who answered my letter-questionnaire, an examination of the information received concerning opportunities in advertising for persons trained in foreign languages indicates that the range is broad, the number of opportunities great, and the financial rewards attractive. The following quotation from the letter of Vaughn M. Bryant, Publicity Director of International House, New Orleans, offers a good general statement on the subject:

"My experience has always been in newspaper work and in this connection there are many opportunities for persons trained in foreign languages. . . . A trained newspaperman who knows a foreign language has an opportunity to go on a paper because that foreign language facility gives him an excellent advantage over other applicants for the job. . . .

"There is also opportunity in advertising agencies for persons trained in a foreign language. Of course, in all of these companies the foreign language in itself is not enough and the applicant must have skills in some particular field of endeavor, but it is the skill in the foreign language in addition to his other skills which in many cases will enable him to get a job, and a well paying one, over another applicant who does not have those foreign language skills."

Presumably the jobs to which Mr. Bryant refers are in domestic newspaper and advertising work, even though they may lead to service abroad. After pointing out that, in his opinion, the study of language, literature and culture of foreign nations is only of special value to those who want to serve in the foreign field, Eugene Meyer, Publisher of *The Washington Post,* makes a statement which seems to include reporters not specifically assigned to foreign posts. He writes: "I am afraid not enough people are being educated in this country in foreign languages, a knowledge which I consider essential for reporters and our diplomatic and commercial foreign representatives."

It is also of interest that in a letter received from Mrs. Eleanor Roosevelt the foreign press is mentioned as the first field of opportunity for persons trained in foreign languages. She states that "people trained in foreign languages can find opportunities in the field of the foreign press and as translators." In view of the world-wide nature of the activities of the American press, the value of foreign language preparation would seem to be almost too obvious to mention for reporters and many other servants of the press, both at home and abroad.

Yet the value of such preparation can hardly be said to receive serious emphasis in the educational programs of those planning to enter the field.

As for the nature of the opportunities reported in advertising, Lyle W. Funk, of Batten, Barton, Durstine and Osborne, says that the greatest opportunities in advertising, for personnel trained in foreign languages, probably lie in translating and writing copy in a foreign language. After speaking of publications in this country printed in foreign languages as a possible market for personnel skilled in foreign languages, Mr. Funk makes a statement concerning salary range which offers strong support for the utility of foreign languages in combination with other skills. He estimates that the salary range "lies between $3000 and $5000, but if these translators also have training in writing advertising copy, they might earn from $6,000 to $10,000.

Public Relations

The powerful impetus given in recent years to the field of public relations is constantly bringing into existence new opportunities in that field. Here again the range is very broad, since it embraces the work of industrial and business divisions in industrial relations, personnel relations, the more recently stressed human relations, and public relation functions of individuals and groups for cities, states, small businesses and colleges. In its more recent aspects, the field of public relations offers a whole new field of opportunity, both in this country and abroad. To return to the letter of Vaughn M. Bryant of International House, New Orleans, one can easily see the link between some phases of public relations and contacts of American business abroad. Mr. Bryant reports: "In the field of public relations, there is constantly need by American companies for trained newspapermen who also know a language who can go abroad in public relations work whether those companies be construction, transportation, petroleum or any of a dozen other classifications. From personal experience, I know that there are good public relations opportunities in such areas as Latin America for persons with news skill and language skill."

This preference of employers in the field of public relations for persons with experience in newspaper work is frequently expressed in the letters received from executives in public relations. It is a natural preference, yet such experience is only an aspect of the desired background.

Most business and industrial firms maintain some division of publicity, whether it be called the advertising department, the public relations division, or some other term. The tremendous range of American business makes this area of opportunity particularly important. As an example of one type of such industrial activity, Carl A. Sundberg, Secretary of the American Locomotive Company, explains: "In this particular field the Foreign and Public Relations Divisions of our organization maintain ample personnel and programs to promote our sales and good will. We have representation in those countries which we feel are most advantageous to our interests, as well as the distribution of technical data, and printed articles in a few foreign language publications."

John Rusinko, Assistant Advertising Manager of the Minneapolis-Moline Company, reports opportunities in the Advertising Department for the preparation or editing of copy for ads in foreign publications, and for the preparation or editing of international material or sales promotion folders. He lists the salary range as $2500 to $7500.

Charles C. Mentzer, of the Employee Relations Division of the International General Electric Company, speaks of a small translation section maintained by his company. The principal work of this department is to translate advertising and publicity material into Spanish for distribution in South America. The few references just made to the field of public relations may suffice to support the statement that the range of opportunity is very broad. The role of foreign language in preparation for the field is an important one; in many phases of the work it is essential.

The employment abroad of American personnel at the higher levels of management by American magazines is worthy of mention. John G. Nesbitt, of the Office of International Editions of the *Reader's Digest*, reports: "As our main dependence on knowledge of languages other than English results from the fact that our United States edition is translated into ten languages, we require that our editorial and translation staffs be people of bilingual ability in English and one of these ten languages." Although these staffs are selected from nationals on the scene of publication abroad, some American executives are found in the foreign offices of the eighteen International Editions. Most of these persons are specialists in matters of production, distribution, or over-all management. No salary range was quoted by Mr. Nesbitt, but another magazine which publishes editions abroad offers some detail concerning executive personnel hired in the United States.

Two positions are mentioned, Business Manager and Assistant Business Manager. The Business Manager has complete charge of the operation of his bureau, including printing of the magazine, distribution to the various countries, advertising sales and promotion, newsstand and subscription sales and promotion, subscription fulfillment, and accounting. The personnel sent out from the United States receive a living allowance in addition to the salary. The salary of a Business Manager may run anywhere from $6000 to $12,000 a year, depending on former experience, length of service, size of the operation, etc., while a living allowance may be from $100 a month to $100 a week, depending on currency exchange and general conditions in the country in which the Manager lives.

Alice L. Barnes, Personnel Manager for *Time,* calls attention to a "Letter from the Publisher" in which the claim is made that 85% of the researchers of the organization speak one or more foreign languages. Miss Barnes also mentions that the head of *Time* Research wants researchers in the Latin America section to have at least a reading knowledge of Spanish.

A few words concerning positions in radio and television are in order. Elliott M. Sanger, Executive Vice President of the *New York Times* station, WQXR and WQXR-FM, believes that in the field of radio, education in liberal arts, including foreign languages, and of course English, are of great importance. He finds "an extensive knowledge of English and a working knowledge of the modern foreign languages" to be of great help to announcers, continuity writers and the program staff, generally.

Doris Ann, Placement Manager of the National Broadcasting Company, points out that although training in foreign languages is not a specific requirement for any of the jobs at NBC, "there are some positions which in addition to specialized radio or television training and experience, require broad cultural experience." In such jobs, knowledge of foreign languages and foreign cultures would augment other qualifications. Miss Ann writes: "the degree of advantage depends on the degree of ability in the individual." She enclosed a 17-page *Job Inventory* for NBC, with the following positions checked: Librarian, Producer—Radio, Production Director—Television, Program Analyst, Public Affairs Director, Sales Account Executive, Station Representative, Writer (Advertising, News, Press, Script, Sports).

Generally it would seem that the broad education in the liberal arts, including foreign languages and cultural studies, is the one most likely to enhance the future of the individual, provided technical requirements are met. Whether the importance of foreign language study in radio and television work is placed on this broad basis, or on the basis of specific vocational use, the fact remains that foreign languages are important in the preparation of employees in radio.

SECRETARIAL POSITIONS

Secretarial positions for persons who add foreign language skills to secretarial skills are reported as commonly available in almost every major type of American business and industry. It is possible to make this statement partly because practically every important type of business in the nation has some contact with foreign areas, either through export or through import. The extent and the importance of this contact is too little recognized by those who determine the nature of curricula designed to prepare secretaries and other business personnel. Firms which would not feel justified in hiring a person for the sole purpose of handling translation of foreign correspondence will frequently hire a person with both secretarial and language skills. The secretary who can compose business letters in the foreign language is even more valuable and favored. Foreign language stenographers have better opportunities for jobs in competitive situations, receive higher pay, and have better chances of advancement to more important positions. These conclusions are based directly on information offered by employers located in all sections of the United States.

The opportunities for employment in this general category reported are not confined to the large urban centers. Since there is less competition in smaller cities, the latter often provide the most favorable market for secretarial personnel. Neither are such jobs confined to business firms with foreign contacts. Many Chambers of Commerce maintain foreign language stenographers as a regular part of their service. Large hotels often offer a similar service. Banks frequently need foreign language stenographers, even when they do not maintain a foreign department. Insurance companies report the need of language trained personnel in such departments as the Policyholders Service Division. Airline and steamship agencies and travel bureaus also need such personnel. The largest market for such personnel is to be found in banking or business houses which have divisions especially interested in the transaction of business with interests abroad.

In this connection, note the following quotation from the letter of B. B. Bowen, Assistant Vice President of the Union Planters

National Bank and Trust Company, Memphis, Tennessee: "Since the United States is now the creditor nation of the world, and much correspondence is carried on between nations, a knowledge of foreign languages is very important. Any concern, whether a bank, a travel bureau, or maybe a government office that maintains a foreign department has a need of the person with a knowledge of foreign languages. In the large banks, they employ a number of men to translate and write letters in foreign languages. . . . In our department, one of our secretaries has a knowledge of French and Spanish. Hardly a day passes that she isn't called upon to translate letters that we receive from foreign countries. Even outsiders, knowing our facilities, bring in their correspondence from foreign countries, therefore making this young lady's knowledge a valuable asset to the bank."

E. C. Earle, Assistant Vice President of the Bankers Trust Company, New York, writes: "We employ two or three bilingual secretaries. They must be able to converse fluently and take dictation accurately. Since the supply of girls with this ability is limited, their services are at a premium, which is reflected in their pay. We also employ several translators, who take care of any incoming mail which is not in English."

Most of the starting salaries reported ranged from $160 per month to $250. In a few cases, higher salaries were indicated. T. C. Ballagh, of Ballagh and Thrall, Export Sales Managers, offers useful advice to persons seeking secretarial positions in foreign trade: "With women, the greatest need is for stenographic ability. Some students feel that they can become translators or interpreters in export offices after several years of college Spanish or French without a knowledge of either shorthand or typing. This is not the case. . . . I always urge students of foreign languages who intend to go into the export business to learn shorthand and typing. This applies to men as well as women. There is no quicker way to learn any business than through the dictation of someone else who knows it. With this opportunity to learn, the person who starts in as a stenographer becomes a secretary, then an assistant, and eventually is able to carry on certain phases of the business without direction until finally he teaches others."

Whether a person starts as stenographer or secretary, with the proper combination of secretarial skills and adequate training in foreign languages, the opportunities are many and the possibilities of advancement excellent.

Opportunities in many phases of banking activities were reported. Starting with such job types as bilingual secretaries, the range of opportunity was extended to include important posts in international banking operations. E. C. Earle, Assistant Vice President of the Bankers Trust Company, New York City, speaks of this kind of opportunity: "Of course, any bank that actively cultivates foreign business needs people with language ability. For example, we employ representatives who travel abroad and for whom the language ability is indispensable. Opportunities in this type of activity offer the greatest chance in the banking field, but . . . it involves very much more than the language ability itself. In other words, the successful man must combine a thorough understanding of commercial banking in this country with methods and practices in the foreign country which he attempts to cultivate."

Peter D. Hanssen, Assistant Cashier, Operations Officer, Bank of America, San Francisco, reports that language skills are "most assuredly considered" among the qualifications of a person applying for foreign service. "Undoubtedly, as time goes on," he says, "the knowledge of languages will become even more important, and perhaps it will become a mandatory qualification for those applying and being trained for work in our foreign branches." Of course, monetary theory and international banking are essential studies in any preparation for positions in the foreign department of a bank.

Firms like the American Express Company may not be recognized by the general public as banking enterprises. Concerning this firm, B. W. Van Riper, Manager of the Educational Travel Division, writes: "The American Express Company is a large and multifarious institution. It is, among other things, an enormous banking system. For that, obviously, training in accounting is valuable. . . . Certainly we have to have men in the office here who can carry on correspondence in all the important languages."

Some commonly overlooked fields of opportunity have been brought to light. The qualifications for one of the most interesting are as follows: A broad, cultural background, an excellent preparation in several languages, a good knowledge of the business, economic and cultural patterns to be found in the areas where the languages are spoken. The duties of such a person would consist of keeping himself informed from day to day of changes, real and potential, which might affect the interests of his employer, and his employer's product.

Such a man would spearhead any efforts of the company to analyze foreign markets, help devise plans to sustain present markets, or assist in developing new markets. Although many or all of these duties may fall to persons already employed for such purposes, many letters received have outlined the need for a specialist fully capable of handling the duties just described.

In the field of consumer goods, firms which manufacture necessities for export offer greater opportunities than others. Special attention needs to be given the great increase in the number of opportunities available in firms which manufacture biological and pharmaceutical supplies. Since the former source of such supplies from Europe has been cut off in great measure, American firms have made great strides in this field.

Manufacturers of heavy machinery, engineering and construction firms offering special technical services present more and better opportunities to persons who qualify with language-technical or the language-management combinations.

All students taking language work are reminded that their opportunity for vocational use of foreign language skills will increase decidedly in proportion to the addition of skills and abilities in other fields. Like some stenographic and secretarial posts, positions in translating and even in interpreting are not too well paid, in comparison with opportunities in other fields. However, the person having a combination of skills, as has been suggested, will find himself well qualified for an attractive position in business.

EMPLOYMENT IN GOVERNMENT

DEPARTMENT OF AGRICULTURE

IN A STATEMENT prepared by A. Rex Johnson, Director of the Office of Foreign Agricultural Relations, on the training and selection of officers for foreign service, three categories of recruitment are mentioned. First of all, the Foreign Service Act, which became effective in November, 1946, provides for the selection of agricultural officers through regular examinations conducted by the Department of State. The other two categories consist of the Foreign Service Reserve Corps (to which persons may be appointed for a period not to exceed four years) and the permanent Foreign Service Staff Corps. Although only a few agricultural officers have been stationed abroad under each of these three categories, Mr. Johnson says that the Department of Agriculture expects an increased number of properly qualified men to be recruited.

A few commodity specialists are sent abroad by the Department of Agriculture on funds made available under provisions of the Research and Marketing Act of 1946. Their responsibility, as described by Mr. Johnson, is to study possible foreign markets for U. S. commodities in plentiful supply. The nature of the majority of foreign assignments is clarified as follows: "Most agricultural assignments abroad are of a general nature, but occasionally the assignment of a highly trained technician is required, usually for a temporary period. It is the more general type of assignment to which new Foreign Service officers are directed." The following list of tasks of the agricultural officer will illustrate the broad, general nature of his work. He may, on assignment: "negotiate or help negotiate with the foreign government; on request, advise and assist in representing the United States at agricultural, food or related conferences and meetings in the country to which he is accredited; give lectures and addresses at agricultural schools, farm societies, etc.; be the chief or close adviser of the United States section on food and agriculture in occupied countries; study, collaborate or advise upon local experimental undertakings, educational projects or other developments; cooperate with officers responsible for student and technical exchanges; exchange seeds, plants, publications, etc., with local officials and agriculturists; act as friend, guide and mentor for a flood of visiting American officials, dignitaries, and private agriculturists."

It is inconceivable that a man whose duties in a foreign nation are so varied could serve effectively without adequate knowledge of the language of that nation as well as of other elements in that nation's culture. It is assumed that he would be: "Possessed with the ability to read the English language with clear understanding and the ability to write with clarity and precision. . . . Reasonably fluent in the use of at least one foreign language."

After suggesting that the best candidate for the position of agricultural officer would be one who has a Master's degree, or even a Doctorate in Agricultural Economics, Mr. Johnson mentions as a more possible combination "some five years' college study of a well-rounded nature, but with at least two full years of basic agricultural courses." The need for more fully prepared candidates for positions and a longer course of study has been emphasized in practically every field of employment represented in this study.

In view of the dissatisfaction expressed with the training of candidates for positions in many fields, it is perhaps of interest to offer the following quotation from the statement enclosed with Mr. Johnson's letter: "The Department of Agriculture is ready to go forward in its cooperation with Land-Grant and other colleges, but it must be emphasized that few agriculturally trained men have been able to pass the foreign service examination."

Agricultural specialists are often selected on a temporary basis and brought into the Reserve Corps. Such senior officers are appointed for a period not exceeding four years, whereas the younger officers are recruited for career service through regular Foreign Service examinations.

The salary range reported for the position of Agricultural Officer is the same as that of Foreign Service Officer of the Department of State. The entrance salary is $3300, plus living allowances while abroad, with periodic promotions possible to a ceiling of $13,500. There are also retirement features. The announcement for the 1949 examinations for Foreign Service Officer states that a candidate must be at least 21 and under 31 years of age as of July 1, 1949. Presumably senior officers for the Reserve Corps are not subject to this ceiling on age.

Up to this point, I have stressed the material enclosed with Mr. Johnson's letter. To return to his letter, the following quotation is pertinent: "The only persons whom we are able to employ are those with technical agricultural training for assignment to various technical stations or missions throughout the world. In such cases, technical competence is of more importance than language facility."

This is to say that the Department of Agriculture is concerned primarily with the smaller number of specialists, while the larger number of persons employed—Mr. Johnson has referred to them as the "generalists"—will be recruited by the Department of State as Foreign Service Officers. Because of the emphasis on technical competence, Mr. Johnson closes his letter saying that foreign language is "important as a vehicle but not important in and of itself." Yet the importance of foreign languages and the broad liberal background in the training of foreign agricultural officers is amply demonstrated by the list of possible duties quoted and by the specific statements concerning the need for an adequate knowledge of English and of foreign languages.

BUREAU OF THE CENSUS

Nathan Habib, Chief of the Shipping Statistics Section of the Foreign Trade Division, Bureau of the Census, offers first the following positive statement: "I can assure you that languages are indispensable in the field of international economics, foreign trade, and transportation."

The following statements by Mr. Habib reveal some aspects of the situation in several areas of government service: "In the government, no special attempt is made in economics or statistics to require specific training in foreign languages. However, an individual's ability to read a foreign language is accepted as an added asset which enables one to make a greater contribution to his work in a particular field. In the fields of international economics, statistics, and transportation, languages are indispensable in enabling one to engage in planning and policy programs."

Mr. Habib goes on to point out how difficult it is to understand the transportation system of a nation without being able to read the language of that nation; in fact, the knowledge of several foreign languages seems to be indispensable to such an understanding. A further reference to Mr. Habib's informative letter discloses a situation commonly found during World War II: "In my work with the United States Maritime Commission during the war, it was quite apparent that very few trained economists and statisticians were versed in foreign languages, and yet correspondence in foreign languages would be assigned to members of the staff at high levels in order to translate and handle official business."

THE CIVIL SERVICE COMMISSION

In view of the key role played by the Civil Service Commission in government employment, the following statement by W. A. McCoy, Chief of the Examining and Placement Division, merits rather full quotation. Mr. McCoy refers only to "positions in the government which require a knowledge of foreign languages as a tool," and not of positions in which foreign languages would be a valuable addition to the general training of the individual. He says:

"The government has comparatively few positions for which skill in a foreign language is a definite requirement in the published announcement, aside from such positions as Translator, Interpreter, or Teacher in the few positions of high school level. Examinations have been held for bilingual stenographers but such positions are more common in war time than under ordinary circumstances. There are, however, a number of positions for which applicants with skill in a particular language or group of languages are requested. Such positions are Intelligence Specialists, Foreign Affairs Analyst, Research Analyst, and Advisor in Education and Librarian for certain positions. The majority of these positions are in the State Department and War and Navy. The Departments of Agriculture, Commerce, and Labor have recently had positions in line with their usual activities, chiefly in statistical and economic fields, which require a good knowledge of various languages as well as various fields of research to interpret and explain the policies of the foreign region in these fields. The physical sciences and engineering have very few requests for applicants with a linguistic background.

"In many positions there are occasional requests for language ability, e.g., it is usually requested that a Forest Ranger in the Southwest have a knowledge of Spanish—or Mexican. In general, the better salaries go to persons who can command two or more languages. Within the last few years there have been a number of requests for Russian, Oriental languages, or a combination, and for Modern Greek."

Special attention should be given to the reference to the increased demand for bilingual secretaries during war time. Such an increase is, at least in part, a natural result of the greater recognition in war time of a continuing need for foreign languages in a wide variety of positions. Bilingual stenographers perform work similar to that of other stenographers, except that they take and transcribe their notes in more than one language. They usually enter the Federal service at salaries of $2724 per year.

The announcement that the Civil Service Commission will accept until further notice applications for the positions of Intelligence Research Specialist, Military Intelligence Specialist, and Foreign Affairs Officer is of special interest to teachers and others who have a good knowledge of foreign languages and political, economic, social and cultural conditions and trends in foreign areas. Graduate study and experience in research and direction of research are important among the qualifications for these positions. The salary range is $3,825 to $6,400 a year (Grades 7, 9, 11 and 12).

Harry B. Mitchell, of the Civil Service Commission, stresses the positions of Social Science Analyst, Economist, Geologist, Librarian, and Educational Specialist. These positions are within the salary range of $2,974 to $10,305 a year and are mentioned as offering some interest and opportunity to persons trained in foreign languages. Since salaries change and examinations for various fields are opened and closed to applicants from time to time, any person interested in such positions should seek the latest information concerning these matters from his local post office or from the United States Civil Service Commission.

Other types of employment less commonly mentioned are: patrol inspector trainee (Immigration and Naturalization Service), scientific or engineering document analyst, research engineer, physicist, chemist, and some positions in customs. War conditions will undoubtedly bring many new needs; almost all will favor the person with a knowledge of foreign languages.

DEPARTMENT OF COMMERCE

The primary requirement for professional positions in the Bureau of Foreign and Domestic Commerce is that the employee be a qualified economist. Juanita L. Jackson, Chief of the Placement Section, Office of Personnel Administration, Department of Commerce, points out that twenty-four hours of study in economics and three hours of statistics are necessary in order to qualify for the Economist option of the Junior Professional Assistant examination given by the U. S. Civil

Service Commission. The importance of English is recognized by Miss Jackson: "Advanced economist positions require experience in economic research and analysis, with demonstrated ability to write acceptably for publication. Effective use of the English language is a valuable asset in any position."

Miss Jackson calls attention to positions in the Patent Office of the Department of Commerce which might escape the attention of some language students. These positions, which pay $4479.60 to a maximum of $6235.20, are for Translators who have "an adequate vocabulary of technical terms in French or German and one other language, and an understanding of the theories involved in various patents in order to render translations in good idiom for the use of the Examiners in the Patent Office." Furthermore, positions as Classifiers of Foreign Patents (Translators), require the language qualifications mentioned above and also the ability to evaluate patents and route them to their proper destinations in the Patent Office. These positions pay $3351 to a maximum of $4479.60. Because a technical background is required for these positions, Miss Jackson writes that "courses in applied science in the fields of physics and chemistry, and practical courses in chemical, electrical, civil, mechanical, mining, or metallurgical engineering are useful." She also feels that a knowledge of the foreign language and culture of an area is valuable in certain positions in the Office of International Trade.

Ruth T. Blond, Secretary to John W. Evans, Director of the Commodities Division, Office of International Trade, writes that the Commodities Division does not require of its specialists the knowledge of any foreign language. Yet the value of foreign languages to such specialists is noted in the following excerpt from her letter: "It is acknowledged that while it would be very helpful for our analysts to be able to read foreign periodicals, reports and specifications in order to get the technical factors covered or the economic analyses or theories presented, still the emphasis must be placed on the knowledge of the commodities."

In further regard to commodity specialists, it is appropriate to round out the picture of their work by quoting from the letter of Lynn R. Edminster, Vice Chairman of the United States Tariff Commission. This statement should be of special interest to schools of commerce and to all those who prepare persons in economic and technical fields: "Knowledge of the English language is vitally important in our work. We need not only first class technicians and commodity specialists to cover the vast range of products encompassed in the Commission's work; but in addition, because of the large volume of reports, surveys, and other written material which we prepare, we need experts who can write clearly and succinctly. Knowledge of foreign languages is likely to be helpful, particularly in connection with the review of foreign publications containing information regarding foreign industry and economic conditions in foreign countries. Much work has been done by the Commission on a series of publications regarding trade and other economic aspects of our relations with the Latin American countries, and a knowledge of Spanish is especially helpful in this connection. It goes without saying that a knowledge of the cultural products of other countries is useful."

The letter of Clarence I. Blau, Acting Director of the Areas Division, Office of International Trade, is also worthy of note: "I should like to emphasize that when people are employed for area work a good reading knowledge and a fair speaking knowledge of one or more languages used in the area in which the applicant intends to specialize is very desirable. If, in addition, the applicant is familiar with the culture, economy and economic history of such country or countries, his opportunity is by that much enhanced."

Foreign languages seem to deserve a continuing place of importance in the preparation of the prospective employee of the Commerce Department.

DEPARTMENT OF STATE

Because of the number of persons employed and the variety of positions involved in the work of the Department of State, it deserves an important place in this analysis. Although the positions of Foreign Service Reserve Officer, Foreign Service Officer, and positions in the Foreign Service Staff Corps have previously been mentioned under the heading of the Department of Agriculture, the Foreign Service of the United States offers a good point of beginning.

Joseph C. Green, Executive Director, Board of Examiners for the Foreign Service, after reminding me that he was limiting his remarks to the relation of modern language study to preparation for the career of Foreign Service Officer, closes his letter with the following summarizing statement: "A reading ability of at least one of five specified modern languages is a requirement for appointment as Foreign Service Officer. Ability to speak and understand a foreign language is not required for appointment, but it is tested in the Oral Examination and due credit is given to those candidates who can demonstrate such ability." In addition to the initial foreign language requirement mentioned by Mr. Green, it should be remembered that, if the other qualifications are present, the more foreign languages an officer can handle, and the greater his fluency in them, the better equipped he is for the work of the Service.

Although no formal examination is held for Foreign Service Reserve Officers—who are assigned on a temporary basis—written, oral and physical examinations are held by those who seek appointment as Foreign Service Officers. The qualifications also include the ability to use the English language as an instrument for clear thinking and fluent but exact composition, the ability to read English rapidly and with accuracy and comprehension, and the ability to write and compose well. Furthermore, the Foreign Service Officer must be highly trained in oral English. In addition to broad understanding in History, Government and Economics, the candidate should have the broadest possible cultural background and adequate knowledge of the history, development and current characteristics of the United States, with particular attention to factors involved in contemporary international relations. Special programs of study based upon some one area of the world, such as the Soviet Union, Japan, China, Southeast Asia, India, or the Near East, are favorably regarded by the examiners.[1] Graduate study is not required, since entrance examinations are geared to a level of academic achievement within the reach of persons holding only the bachelor's degree. The age group is twenty-one to thirty-one. The salary level ranges from $3300 to $4400 per year, with quarters allowances abroad, travel expenses under orders, cost-of-living allowances at some posts, and possible promotion eventually to classes paying up to $13,500.

Judson H. Lightsey, Chief, Recruitment Section, Division of Foreign Service Personnel and A. Cyril Crilley, Chief, Division of Foreign Reporting Services, enclosed with their letters materials concerning the Foreign Service Staff Corps. This group, Mr. Lightsey states,

[1] The educational requirements briefly summarized above deserve careful consideration, since dozens of letters from business executives referred to the requirements of the Foreign Service as being ideal for many positions in the business world. One example of such references is found in the letter of Arthur A. Verner, Sales Manager, Export Division, The Kelly-Springfield Tire Company. After pointing up specific qualifications in fields such as engineering, he goes on to say that "in the general field of sales, the educational background requirements may not be as specific; therefore, I would say that any course of study patterned after the current State Department requirements, as set forth in their annual examination, would be quite adequate general training."

might be said to comprise the rank and file of the Foreign Service, as well as a number of more advanced personnel in administrative and technical positions. He goes on to say that "although it is quite apparent that ability to use modern languages with facility is of great value to anyone contemplating a career in the Foreign Service, it is not considered to be a qualifying factor of primary importance in the Staff Corps, aside from the exceptions noted. . . ." The more interesting exceptions noted follow:

"There are from time to time openings for persons who have a thorough knowledge of an unusual language such as Arabic, Rumanian, Finnish, Polish, Bulgarian, Hungarian, Icelandic, Serbo-Croatian, Czech, or better known dialects of other languages, and who have training and experience in one of the following occupations: stenographer, typist, administrative clerk, file clerk, telephone operator, accounting clerk, translator, or interpreter. General requirements for Staff Employee appointments apply to these positions, except that the age limit for qualified interpreters and translators is 21 to 46, and in exceptional circumstances waivers of the requirement that candidates be single may be granted. Salaries range from $2850 to $3210 for clerical positions, and from $3210 to $3930 for interpreters and translators. In addition to the clerical aptitude tests, applicants must pass a language examination.

"There are occasional openings for persons who are experienced in the cultural, informational and public affairs fields and librarians and other similar personnel for positions related to the informational and cultural aspects of the Foreign Service. To be favorably considered for such appointments, applicants must have a broad background of pertinent experience and a good working knowledge of a foreign language."

Other divisions of the Department of State also stress the value of a knowledge of foreign languages. Cleon O. Swayzee, Chief, Division of International Labor and Social Affairs, writes: "This Division feels very strongly that persons doing labor reporting in foreign missions should have a good working facility in the language of the country of assignment." W. Walton Butterworth, Director for Far Eastern Affairs at the time of his reply to my letter, calls the knowledge of the language of the foreign country with which a political officer is dealing "highly desirable." After writing of the "important contribution" which persons trained in foreign languages can make in the research division of the Department, where knowledge of particular foreign languages is essential, Mr. Butterworth speaks of "tremendous opportunities for service abroad in the United States Foreign Service establishments."

After recommending strongly the combination of language and area studies now being organized as part of the curriculum in certain leading American universities, Mr. Butterworth calls attention to the important role of language experts in the Division of Language Services.

An especially complete summary of the work of the Division of Language Services has been prepared by officers of that Division. If the following quotation seems long, one must remember that it is only a brief sample of a larger source of pertinent information furnished by Guillermo A. Suro, Chief, Division of Language Services. It will be of special interest to those who are interested in positions as translators or interpreters:

"The opportunities for persons trained in languages with which I am most familiar are those existing in the United States Government service or in international organizations. Undoubtedly you have already been in touch with such organizations as the United Nations, UNESCO, the Organization of American States (including the Pan American Union), the Pan American Sanitary Bureau, the Food and Agriculture Organization of the United Nations, and other similar bodies. All of these require personnel with language knowledge, including bilingual and trilingual stenographers, editorial specialists with a reading knowledge of languages, translators, and interpreters. You are probably also acquainted with the part played by interpreters and translators at the trials of war criminals held at Nuremberg and in Japan. In Washington there are often openings in foreign diplomatic missions for persons with language knowledge.

"Translators are found throughout the Government service but the most important groups are in the State Department, the Library of Congress, the Veteran's Administration, the Central Intelligence Agency, and the Departments of the Army and the Navy.

"As anyone interested in languages realizes, even a superficial knowledge of a foreign language is of value in a wide variety of positions. One of the first important points of contact, however, between language knowledge and another specialized field is in the editorial field. In this Division, for example, editors are employed who must first of all understand publishing but who must also have a fair reading knowledge of one or more foreign languages. Next in order, so far as extent of knowledge of language required is concerned, are bilingual and trilingual stenographers. Printers also fall in this category. At the translator level, qualifications vary according to the needs of various agencies and concerns. In this Division, translations are prepared of a wide variety of important documents, such as treaties, and agreements, diplomatic notes, legal papers, laws and regulations, material for international conferences, communications between heads of state, captured war documents, important addresses, and informational material for distribution abroad. Many of these translations are the basis on which diplomatic action is taken. A large percentage of them are published. Therefore, translators must be expert not only in the languages or language from which they are translating but in the language in which the translation appears. The translations must convey exactly the meaning and spirit of the original, and in addition be idiomatic, grammatically correct, readable, and complete. Therefore, all training which leads to good literary style is important.

"Since the material translated covers many fields, translators must have a broad background of education and experience, preferably in such fields as political science and economics. When translations of highly technical material are required, it is customary to have the translation prepared on a contract basis by outside translators who have a specialized knowledge of the field covered.

"Interpreters must have not only an expert knowledge of two or more languages and broad educational backgrounds but a special flair for interpreting which some people are unable to acquire."

The emphasis upon the importance of the knowledge of English, the ability to edit, and training which leads to good literary style is especially worthy of note.

Evidence of the Federal Government's need for persons fully and properly trained in foreign languages and in specific problems of the inter-relation of the political, economic and social institutions of the area in which the language is spoken can be found in the very fact that a Foreign Service Institute has been created to aid in such training. Before entering into a description of the work of the Institute, Henry Lee Smith, Jr., Director, School of Language Training, Foreign Service Institute, offers this general picture of the nature of the service rendered:

"The Foreign Service Institute through its Schools of Language Training and Advanced Officer Training is engaged in training language and area specialists to serve at the more important East European and Asiatic posts. This is done through a combination of courses at the Institute, at cooperating colleges and universities, and through programs set up by the Institute in the field. The Institute is also engaged in less intensive language instruction in up to forty languages in Washington and in the field and in intensive courses and tutorials in linguistic science."

BUREAU OF INTERNAL REVENUE

Eldon P. King, Special Deputy Commissioner, Bureau of Internal Revenue, calls attention to the field of taxation, in which ability in the use of foreign languages is of particular value. Since this combination is so easily overlooked by persons qualified in the technicalities of taxation, I quote at some length from Mr. King's letter:

"The international field in which my experience lies is that of bilateral international treaties relating to estate and income taxes. This activity has, in the past, involved considerable foreign travel to non-English speaking countries, necessitating the presence of interpreters. In this regard, the revenue service relies upon United States Diplomatic Missions on the ground to furnish the necessary personnel. The subject of taxation is, of course, a highly technical one and thus it is, in practice, rather unlikely to find combined in the same individual knowledge of foreign languages and, at the same time, a sound grasp of legal technicalities of taxation.

"In this field, therefore, a command over one or more additional languages is of considerable value and, when associated in the same individual knowledge of the fundamentals of taxation would be especially valuable to the individual equipped with such qualifications.

"With respect to the opportunities within the Internal Revenue Service for persons qualified in one or more foreign languages, the headquarters of the service are frequently visited by officials of foreign countries and efficient liaison with such officials frequently requires knowledge of a foreign language. In the field of tax research, translation of foreign tax laws is always essential, while the effect of foreign taxation laws is a matter with which the revenue service is frequently called upon to consider in the ordinary administration of its revenue laws."

As Mr. King points out, the service is always glad to have among its personnel a sufficient number of persons whose linguistic abilities are sufficient to meet situations as they arise, yet a person who combines a knowledge of language with a thorough grasp of taxation is not often found. It would seem to be time for an attempt to prepare more persons in this combination of skills.

INSTITUTE OF INTER-AMERICAN AFFAIRS

Marinda R. Barnes, Classification Officer, Personnel Section, Institute of Inter-American Affairs, reports that the staff of the Washington office of that organization is small, and that staff positions are filled by persons who qualify under competitive examinations administered by the Civil Service Commission. On the other hand, employment opportunities in Latin America are exempt from competitive examinations and for the most part include such fields as Public Health, Sanitary Engineering, Hospital Administration, Agriculture, Education (particularly vocational and teacher training), and Business Administration. Experience, ability in a specialized field, and an appropriate degree, ranging from B.S. to Dr. P. H., are necessary for the latter positions. Although the Washington office does not employ language specialists, the Spanish language is essential for many of the jobs in Latin America. Knowledge of Spanish is, however, required only in certain positions where applicants must converse frequently with the Latin Americans.

CENTRAL INTELLIGENCE AGENCY

Several letters were received from Central Intelligence, but one brief quotation from the letter of A. P. Flynn, Chief, Procurement and Placement, Personnel Division, Central Intelligence Agency, will suffice. He writes: "We are always interested in persons with a knowledge of foreign languages and foreign areas. Training in foreign affairs or political science, combined with foreign language ability, is particularly adaptable to our work."

FEDERAL BUREAU OF INVESTIGATION

John Edgar Hoover, Director of the Federal Bureau of Investigation, United States Department of Justice, did not mention any value language training might have with regard to Special Agent personnel. He did, however, make the following remarks about the position of Translator: "The only type of position in this Bureau having proficiency in foreign languages as a prerequisite is that of translator, which is open to either male or female applicants, and the salary grade depends upon the individual qualifications of each applicant, with particular emphasis on the number and difficulty of the foreign languages in which the applicant is proficient, together with his general related experience."

United Nations

Although it would be possible to take up in detail the information received from various international organizations, this section of my report must come to a a close with a few excerpts from the letter of Byron Price, Assistant Secretary-General in charge of Administrative and Financial Services, the United Nations. In the main, only three posts are listed as being of special interest to language students, and these are not at the level of the college graduate. Mr. Price says: "Training in languages is directly relevant to the specifically linguistic posts which we have (mainly interpreters, editors and translators). Translators have to render one or more of the five official languages (English, French, Spanish, Russian and Chinese) into their mother tongue, which must, of course, be one of the official languages." It is interesting to note the following recognition of the translator's need for a knowledge of the foreign culture, in addition to the language: "A knowledge (either academic or gained by experience) of the culture of the foreign countries concerned is an asset, since a translator must know not only the literal meaning of the foreign language, but must be able to catch allusions and references." A knowledge of French and English, the two working languages of the Secretariat, is generally useful but not essential—except in a few positions—for the non-linguistic posts. Spanish was the language mentioned as being next in usefulness.

In general, there are few openings for graduates just out of college (although there are sometimes one or two trainee posts). The most hopeful note in Mr. Price's letter, as far as such persons are concerned, is the following: "We are hoping however gradually to increase our recruitment of young men and women with a good general background, with a view to training them within the organization."

III

FIELDS OF OPPORTUNITY

THE FOLLOWING LIST is made up of the professional fields and divisions of business and industry in which opportunities exist for those who have the necessary combination of skills and abilities.

Accounting
Advertising
Agriculture (technical aspects)
Banking and Finance (domestic; credit, investments, securities)
Banking (international)
Chemical Industry
Clerkships (office and sales)
Coffee (growing, processing, distribution)
Commercial Nucleonics (foreign contacts only)
Construction (engineering aspect as well as manual labor)
Communications (telephone, telegraph and cable)
Dress Designing, Fashions, Perfumes and Cosmetics
Engineering and Technical Positions
Federal Government Service
Film Service and Distribution
Food Canning, Processing and Distribution
Foreign Trade
Geology
Health and Sanitation
Hospital Work
Hotel Work
Industrial Relations
Insurance (all kinds—domestic and foreign)
Journalism (domestic and foreign)
Law (domestic and international aspects)
Library Work
Mail Order Houses
Management

Manufacturing and Marketing of Manufactured Products

air conditioning equipment
aircraft and parts
automobiles
bakery products
beverages (soft drinks, beer, distilled liquors)
building materials (insulation and others)
business and office machines
camera equipment
candy and chewing gum
clothing (including tailoring)
cork products
drug and biological supplies
electrical equipment
electrical medical products
elevator equipment
firearms
fireworks
foundry products
fountain pens
glass and optical instruments
gyroscopes and precision instruments
hardware supplies
heating equipment
heavy machinery; road and farm equipment
home products and household equipment
ink
jewelry
leather processing and leather goods
linoleum products
marine motors
mechanics' tools and supplies
metal, steel and wood products
musical instruments (pianos)
paper containers
petroleum products
pharmaceutical products
pumps
radios, radio supplies and recording equipment
railroad car and locomotive
razor blades
refrigeration equipment
rubber products
scales

    sewing machines
    shoes
    sports equipment
    textiles
    veterinary supplies
    washing machines
    watches
    x-ray equipment
Market Analysis
Meat Packing
Merchandising
Messenger Positions (freight forwarding, diplomatic courier, etc.)
Metal Processing
Mining
Missionary Service
Motion Picture Industry
Music
Plant, Production and Manufacturing Positions
Printing
Professional Opportunities Abroad
Public Relations
Public Service Organization (including welfare, rehabilitation, etc.)
Public Utilities (electric and gas)
Radio and Television
Recording Industry
Research
Sales (domestic and foreign)
Secretarial Positions
Seed Growers and Distributors
Social and Welfare
Statistics
Steel Industry
Sugar Refining
Teaching and Training (academic, technical; domestic and foreign)
Tobacco Industry
Transportation (air, steamship; passenger and freight)
Translation and Interpreting
Travel Agency Positions

IV

A PARTIAL LIST OF REPORTING
EXECUTIVES

THE FOLLOWING is a partial list of contributors of the materials used in this survey. The names of others have been omitted at their own request.

William C. Ackerman, Director, Reference Department, Columbia Broadcasting System, Inc.

D. C. Adams, Manager, Export Department, Addressograph-Multigraph Corporation

Solomon Agoos, Chairman of the Board, Allied Kid Company

R. F. Ahrens, Vice President, United Air Lines

R. J. Aitchison, President, Fansteel Metallurgical Corporation

Roger Albright, Director, Educational Services, Motion Picture Association of America

Carl E. Alfaro, President, International Brass and Copper Company

Gordon W. Allport, Department of Social Relations, Harvard University

E. W. Amardeil, Manager, Foreign Banking Department, Whitney National Bank of New Orleans

S. Amdisen, Secretary and Treasurer, Atlas Imperial Diesel Engine Company

Anthony Anable, Director of Personnel, The Dorr Company

G. V. Anderson, Director, Industrial Relations, Mergenthaler Linotype Company

L. N. Anderson, Assistant to the Executive Vice President, Mackay Radio and Telegraph Company, Inc.

J. Andreoli, Executive Vice President, General Tire and Rubber Export Company

Doris Ann, Placement Manager, National Broadcasting Company

A. F. Armstrong, Staff Employment and Training Supervisor, Scott Paper Company

Viola A. Asselin, Export-Import Manager, Brown and Bigelow Company

Frederick G. Atkinson, Director of Personnel and Industrial Relations, R. H. Macy and Company, Incorporated

Arthur W. Ayers, Manager of Personnel Relations, American Viscose Corporation

B. L. Babcock, Treasurer, Endicott Johnson Corporation

E. M. Bailey, Manager, Export Division, A. E. Staley Manufacturing Company

T. C. Ballagh, Ballagh and Thrall Company

Arthur Barlow, President, The Corn King Company

R. E. Barmeier, Personnel Department, Sears, Roebuck and Company

A. L. Barnard, National Broadcasting Company, Incorporated

Alice L. Barnes, Personnel Manager, *Time,* Incorporated

Marinda R. Barnes, Classification Officer, Personnel Section, Institute of Inter-American Affairs

W. F. Barr, Personnel Manager, Seth Thomas Clocks

Daniel J. Bergen, Public Relations Department, Sun Oil Company

W. R. Bickford, Editor, *Export Trade and Shipper,* Thomas Ashwell and Company, Incorporated

A. W. K. Billings, Jr., Export Manager, Gillette Safety Razor Company

Clarence I. Blau, Acting Director, Area Division, Office of International Trade, Department of Commerce

M. H. Blodgett, Pesonnel Department, Merrill, Lynch, Pierce, Fenner and Beane

Ruth T. Blond, Secretary to John W. Evans, Director of the Commodities Division, Office of International Trade, Department of Commerce

Edward C. Boggs, Manager, Export Division, The Parker Pen Company

H. H. Bohlman, Export Manager, The Seamless Rubber Company

Leo H. Bombard, Assistant Secretary, Guaranty Trust Company of New York

Robert L. Boughton, Export Manager, The White Motor Company

B. B. Bowen, Assistant Vice President, Union Planters National Bank and Trust Company, Memphis, Tennessee.

J. H. Boyd, Manager, The International Free Trade Zone No. 2

R. L. Bracken, Export Manager, Millers Falls Company

F. Kenneth Brasted, Director, Education Department, National Association of Manufacturers

John A. Brogan, Jr., King Features Syndicate

Francis J. Brown, Staff Associate, American Council on Education

Vaughn M. Bryant, Publicity Director, International House, New Orleans

W. J. Burke, Vice President, American Car and Foundry Export Company

Lloyd G. Butler, Export Manager, Harris-Seybold Company

W. Walton Butterworth, Director, Far Eastern Affairs, Department of State

Charles S. Campbell, President, The J. B. Williams Company

James S. Carson, Chairman, Foreign Trade Education Committee, National Foreign Trade Council, Incorporated

R. G. Carter, Abbott Laboratories International Company

T. B. Catron, Vice President, McCormick Overseas Trading Company

Donald Chadduck, Director Overseas Sales, The Carter's Ink Company

W. Howard Chase, Director, Department of Public Relations, General Foods Corporation

Emily H. Chesnut, Director of Personnel, McCall Corporation

General Lucius D. Clay, Retired, U. S. Army

R. C. Clement, Export Department, The Buda Company

C. H. Coats, Export Manager, A. P. Green Fire Brick Company

G. G. Cobean, President, Bulkley, Dunton Paper Company

R. L. Collier, Executive Vice President, Gray Iron Founders' Society, Incorporated

Francis J. Colligan, Chief, Division of International Exchange of Persons, Department of State

Katherine Comstock, Educational Division, Dictaphone Corporation

F. W. Conant, Vice President—Manufacturing, Douglas Aircraft Company, Incorporated

Edward S. Conger, Assistant Secretary, Export-Import Bank of Washington, D. C.

W. N. Cook, President, E. B. Meyrowitz, Incorporated

Charles B. Coursen, Jr., Export Manager, General Biological Supply House

L. G. Coveney, Otis, McAllister and Company

P. H. Crago, Young and Glenn Division, Harvey Watkins Associates, Incorporated

J. B. Cravath, Supervisor, Personnel Department, Standard Oil Company of California

Ann Crawford, Subscription Department, Joshua B. Powers, Incorporated

A. Cyril Crilley, Chief, Division of Foreign Reporting Services, Department of State

Esther D. Cronin, Office Personnel Supervisor, The American Sugar Refining Company

Frances Currier, Secretary, New England Export Club, Incorporated

L. A. Daly, The D. L. Clark Company

Frank D'Aquila, Export Sales Manager, Iowa Manufacturing Company

Dawson F. Dean, Ph.D., Director of Personnel, Executive Offices, American Home Products Corporation

Philip B. Deane, Read Machinery Division, Standard Stoker Company, Incorporated

K. E. Deardorff, Office Manager, Export Department, The Euclid Road Machinery Company

John F. Des Reis, Export Department, Ronson Art Metal Works

Emilio Desvernine, Jr., Publicity Department, Socony-Vacuum Oil Company

I. Dick, President, Dick Coffee Company, Incorporated

George P. Dixon, Vice President, International Telephone and Telegraph Corporation

F. C. Donovan, Employee Relations Department, Standard-Vacuum Oil Company

Walter Dowling, Chargé d'Affaires a. i., The Foreign Service of the United States, American Legation, Vienna, Austria

J. vB. Dresser, Assistant Export Manager, Canada Dry International, Incorporated

Roger R. Dulong, Export Sales Manager, Carter Carburetor Corporation

E. C. Earle, Assistant Vice President, Bankers Trust Company

Henry J. Ebert, Manager, Export Division, Cleaver-Brooks Company

George A. Eckweiler, Export Manager, Noble and Wood Machine Company

Lynn R. Edminster, Vice Chairman, United States Tariff Commission

A. R. Edwards, Director of Distribution, The Armco International Corporation

J. M. Ehni, Export Sales Manager, The DeVilbiss Company

O. J. Ellertson, Export Manager, Pioneer Engineering Works, Incorporated

Amita Ellison, N. Y. Personnel Representative, Marshall Field and Company

Samuel S. Ericsson, Assistant Manager, Foreign Commerce Department, Chamber of Commerce of the United States

Bryant Essick, President, Essick Manufacturing Company

H. G. Evans, Vice President, Hamilton Manufacturing Company

Walter A. Everett, Export Manager, The Deming Company

Irving J. Fain, Apex Tire and Rubber Company

W. C. Fay, Personnel Manager, American Optical Company

R. A. Featherstone, Assistant to the Office Manager, Standard Brands

Julian W. Feiss, Assistant to the Director, Bureau of Mines, U. S. Department of the Interior

N. C. Firth, Editor of "Dun's Review," Dun and Bradstreet, Incorporated

L. J. Fletcher, Director of Training and Community Relations, Caterpillar Tractor Company

A. P. Flynn, Chief, Procurement and Placement, Personnel Division, Central Intelligence Agency

H. W. Francis, Vice President, Francis Metal Products Company

H. W. French, Vice President, The Bridgeport Hardware Manufacturing Corporation

Pete French, President, Pete French and Company

Lyle W. Funk, Batten, Barton, Durstine and Osborne, Incorporated

W. W. Gallagher, Jr., MacGregor Instrument Company

M. G. Garcia, Vice President and General Manager, The Kelley-Koett International Corporation

George Gardner, Educational Director, Pan American World Airways System

R. W. Gifford, Director, Borg-Warner International Corporation

James L. Gilbert, Senior Vice President, McGraw-Hill International Corporation

J. F. Gillen, American President Lines, Ltd.

J. D. Gillespie, Assistant Export Manager, Graflex, Incorporated

L. E. Gillet, Office Manager, American Chicle Company

J. L. Godwin, President, Godwin Shipping Company, Incorporated

Clinton S. Golden, Labor Adviser, Economic Cooperation Administration

J. S. Goldware, Blue Star Foods, Incorporated

Fitzhugh Granger, Merchandising Services, International Harvester Export Company

Mortimer Graves, American Council of Learned Societies

J. C. Green, Executive Director, Board of Examiners for the Foreign Service, Department of State

P. L. Green, Counsellor, Division of Publicity, Pan American Union

Wesley Greene, President, International Film Bureau, Incorporated

Bernard Greenfelder, International Lawyer

R. J. Greenly, Assistant Director of Personnel Relations, Jones and Laughlin Steel Corporation

W. L. Griffith, Employment Manager, Eastern Air Lines

W. F. Haberer, Export Manager, Deere and Company

Nathan Habib, Chief, Shipping Statistics Section, Foreign Trade Division, Bureau of the Census

L. T. Hallett, Chairman, College Recruiting Committee, General Aniline and Film Corporation

A. L. Hammell, President, Railway Express Agency

R. G. Hanna, Export Manager, Gray Marine Motor Company

P. D. Hanssen, Assistant Cashier, Operations Officer, Bank of America, San Francisco

R. G. Harder, Personnel Manager, Asiatic Petroleum Corporation

G. N. Hardesty, Assistant Manager, The Merchants National Bank of Mobile

Helen Mary Harding, Export Manager, The Doall Company

W. Harnischfeger, President, Harnischfeger Corporation

A. W. Harrington, Export Department, Burroughs Adding Machine Company

John Harrison, Personnel Manager, Gulf Oil Corporation

Robin B. Hatfield, Personnel Manager, American President Lines

J. W. Hathaway, Employment Manager, Sharp and Dohme, Incorporated

A. R. Hauschel, Vice President, J. I. Case Company

Henriette Hautefeuille, General Manager, Callot Soeurs of Paris, Incorporated

R. G. Hawley, Sales Manager, College Department, Harper Brothers

W. M. Healy, Manager, Export Sales Department, Rheem Manufacturing Company

W. R. Herstein, Executive Director, Memphis International Center

J. B. Herzog, President, Stern, Morgenthau and Company, Incorporated

G. H. Hieronymus, Chief, Utilization Branch, Department of the Army, Civilian Personnel Division

Tracy Higgins, President, Higgins Ink Company, Incorporated

L. J. Hitch, Export Manager, Virginia Smelting Company

Hugh W. Hitchcock, Director of Advertising and Public Relations, Packard Motor Car Company

Charles J. Hoffman, Export Manager, Gar Wood Industries, Incorporated

Stanley E. Hollis, President, American Foreign Credit Underwriters

John Holmes, President, Swift and Company

J. Edgar Hoover, U. S. Department of Justice, F.B.I.

J. H. Howard, Business and Technical Personnel Director, Eastman Kodak Company

H. S. Hower, Jr., Manager, Corning Glass Works

E. K. Hubbard II, Vice President, United Aircraft Export Corporation

Houlder Hudgins, President, Sloane-Blabon Corporation

J. C. Hussey, Manager, Overseas Division, Royal Typewriter Company, Incorporated

E. C. Hyland, Assistant Manager, Export Sales, The Yale and Towne Manufacturing Company

W. S. Idler, Personnel Department, Aluminum Company of America

Austin S. Igleheart, President, General Foods Corporation

Juanita L. Jackson, Chief, Placement Section, Department of Commerce

J. K. Jenney, Assistant Director, Foreign Relations Department, du Pont de Nemours and Company

Jill Jessee, Promotion Manager, Lenthéric

J. F. Johannsen, Export Manager, Hyster Company

A. Rex Johnson, Assistant Director, U. S. Department of Agriculture

J. L. Johnson, Director of Industrial Relations, International Shoe Company

R. W. Johnson, Chairman of the Board, Johnson and Johnson

W. L. Johnson, Director, Personnel and Industrial Relations, Bell and Howell Company

Edwin L. Jones, President, J. A. Jones Construction Company

Roy S. Jones, Vice President, The Coca-Cola Export Sales Company

Joseph Jorda, Export Manager, The Mennen Company

G. S. Joy, Office Manager, Libby, McNeill and Libby

R. G. Kaiser, Superviser, Education and Training, Merchandising Services, International Harvester Company

A. P. Keeler, Export Manager, The Fuller Brush Company

Eldon P. King, Special Deputy Commissioner, Bureau of Internal Revenue

John Kinsey, Export Manager, Micromatic Hone Corporation

E. Kriegsman, President, Kriegsman Paper Company

Elmer R. Krueger, President, Paper Art Company

L. W. Kullman, Export Manager, The Kilgore Manufacturing Company

F. M. Kurtz, President, American Coffee Corporation

J. A. Lambie, Acting Chief, Salary and Wage Administration Branch, Department of the Army

R. P. Lamont, Vice President, Export Operating Company

M. P. Langdoc, Export Director, Williams Oil-O-Matic Division

E. H. Lankenau, Assistant Vice President, Manufacturers Trust Company

W. G. LaPoe, Assistant Employment Manager, Armstrong Cork Company

A. W. Larson, Manager, Personnel Department, The Goodyear Tire and Rubber Export Company

J. J. Leckie, Sales Promotion Bureau, Pencil Sales Department, Joseph Dixon Crucible Company

W. K. Lentz, Employment Supervisor, National Biscuit Company

S. H. Lewis, Export Sales Department, Easy Washing Machine Corporation

J. H. Lightsey, Chief, Recruitment Section, Division of Foreign Service Personnel, Department of State

A. R. Lillicrapp, Treasurer, Export Manager, Dixie Cup Company

C. W. Linscheid, Manager, Export Division, Fairbanks, Morse and Company, Incorporated

Archie Lochhead, President, Universal Trading Corporation

R. A. Lydy, Director of Foreign Sales, Champion Spark Plug Company

J. MacDonald, Export Manager, The Four Wheel Drive Auto Company

C. E. Mack, Director, Federal Supply Service, General Services Administration, Bureau of Federal Supply

Gustave Mahler, Vice President, Schroder Rockefeller and Company

Ray Manning, Vice President, Director of Sales, Hart, Schaffner and Marx

H. P. Marshall, College Department, Charles Scribner's Sons

W. P. Marshall, President, The Western Union Telegraph Company

R. L. Mason, Manager, Employee Relations Department, Standard Oil Company of New Jersey

J. A. Maxwell, Export Manager, Otis Elevator Company

Harold Mayfield, Industrial Relations Division, Owens-Illinois Glass Company

Fred Maytag III, President, The Maytag Company

D. C. McCarthy, Socony-Vacuum Oil Company

J. J. McCarthy, Assistant General Manager, Gimbel Brothers

G. D. McClaren, Assistant General Personnel Director, Pittsburgh Plate Glass Company

O. P. McComas, Executive Vice President, Phillip Morris and Company, Ltd., Incorporated

Strubbe McConnell, Jr., Manager, Employee Relations, Standard Oil Company of New Jersey

W. A. McCoy, Chief, Examining and Placement Division, U. S. Civil Service Commission

J. F. McCrudden, Export Manager, Aberfoyle Manufacturing Company

G. R. McDermott, Vice President In Charge Foreign Division, Surface Combustion Corporation

J. N. McDonnell, Vice President, Schering Corporation

D. McIntosh, Philco International Corporation

F. F. McManus, Employment Department, United Fruit Company

K. A. Meade, Director, College and University Relations, General Motors Corporation

R. G. Meisenhelder, Assistant to the Personnel Manager, A.B. Farquhar Company

C. C. Mentzer, Employee Relations Division, International General Electric Company

Eugene Meyer, Publisher, *The Washington Post*

V. N. Meyers, Personnel Department, Campbell Soup Company

V. P. Mickelson, The Chesapeake and Ohio Railway Company

B. B. Miller, Manager, Personnel Relations Department, General Electric X-Ray Corporation

R. G. Miller, Vice President, Tracerlab, Incorporated

W. S.   ɪny

A. Mi   *Partial List of Reporting Executives*   elations, Ford International

Harry B. Mitchell, United States Civil Service Commission

T. D. Montgomery, Manager, Foreign Sales, Cutler-Hammer, Incorporated

J. J. Morsman, Jr., Assistant Comptroller, National Lead Company

O. B. Motter, O. B. Motter and Associates

C. S. Moyds, Personnel Director, Ciba Pharmaceutical Products, Incorporated

D. R. Munsick, Sales Manager, Interchemical Corporation

W. LaC. Neilson, Jr., Export Manager, Greenfield Tap and Die Corporation

J. G. Nesbitt, Office of International Editions, *Reader's Digest*

J. D. Nichols, Vice President, Thomas A. Edison, Incorporated

E. J. Noble, Chairman of the Board, American Broadcasting Company, Incorporated

W. C. Nusbaum, N. Y. Sales Division, Tracerlab, Incorporated

Irving S. Olds, Chairman of the Board, U. S. Steel Corporation

J. W. Oram, Chief of Personnel, The Pennsylvania Railroad

R. Ordway, Operating Manager, S. S. Pierce Company

R. E. Oscar, Director of Exports, Maremont Automotive Products, Incorporated

M. N. Palmer, Export Manager, Hickok Manufacturing Company, Incorporated

J. R. Palomo, Export Division, Nash-Kelvinator Corporation

T. I. Parkinson, President, The Equitable Life Assurance Society

F. W. Parmelee, Export Sales Manager, Toledo Scale Company

H. G. Paul, Director of Export Sales, Columbus Coated Fabrics Corporation

J. H. Payne, Export Director, Aircraft Industries Association

A. A. Pearson, Manager, Training Department, Ford Motor Company

Rollin Peck, Export Manager, Arrow-Hart and Hegeman Electric Company

F. L. Pell, Jr., Vice President, The Philadelphia National Bank

M. Perez, Export Manager, Miles Laboratories, Incorporated

A. H. Pfeiffer, Manager of Industrial Relations, Bucyrus-Erie Company

H. C. Phillips, Hercules Powder Company

W. L. Pierson, Chairman of the Board, Trans World Air Lines

M. L. Pilliard, Baz-Dresch, Pilliard and Company

G. S. Pillsbury, Overseas Vice President, Pillsbury Mills, Incorporated

J. B. Potts, Vice President, Manhattan Storage and Warehouse Company

John Powers, Jr., Secretary, Charles Pfizer and Company, Incorporated

E. G. Poxson, General Staff, General Motors Overseas Operations

Byron Price, Assistant Secretary-General, In Charge of Administrative and Financial Services, United Nations

K. A. Redfield, President, Asgrow Export Corporation

P. D. Reed, Chairman of the Board, General Electric Company

V. D. Reed, Assistant Director of Research, J. Walter Thompson Company

Allen Reffler, Manager, Foreign Sales Division, Dun and Bradstreet, Incorporated

Harris Reinhardt, Manager, Employment and Training Division, Industrial Relations Department, Sylvania Electric Products, Incorporated

S. D. Richards, Special Assistant to the Administrator, Economic Cooperation Administration

W. S. Robertson, President, American and Foreign Power Company, Incorporated

W. F. Rockwell, Jr., President, Rockwell Manufacturing Company

R. R. Roger, Manager of Export Sales, Sperry Gyroscope Company

Mrs. Eleanor Roosevelt

Joseph C. Rovensky

G. A. Rowland, Sales Manager, Buflovak Equipment Company

Wade C. Ruble, Manager of Employment, The B. F. Goodrich Company

A. M. Rupkey, Manager of Personnel, Bethlehem Steel Company

John Rusinko, Assistant Advertising Manager, Minneapolis-Moline Company

E. L. Ryerson, Chairman of the Board, Inland Steel Company

Elliott M. Sanger, Executive Vice President, Radio Stations WQXR and WQXR-FM, *New York Times*

F. E. Savale, Industrial Relations Department, Westinghouse Electric International Company

A. F. Scharen, General Manager, International Division, Servel Incorporated

J. T. Schenck, President, The Engelberg Huller Company, Incorporated

M. R. Schoonmaker, Manager, Eastern Region, The Paraffine Companies, Incorporated

Emil Schram, President, The New York Stock Exchange

C. D. Scudder, Jr., Law Department, Brown and Williamson Tobacco Corporation

R. P. Seely, Secretary to R. Stanley Dollar, The Robert Dollar Company

Max Sherover, Director, The Linguaphone Institute

L. W. Shorter, Assistant to General Export Manager, Republic Steel Corporation

H. D. Simpson, Manager, Plated Division, Krementz and Company

H. L. Smith, Jr., Director, School of Language Training, Foreign Service Institute, Department of State

H. Lyman Smith, Director, Foreign Trade Bureau, St. Louis Chamber of Commerce

Philip C. Smith, Vice President, Yardley of London, Inc.

Brehon Somervell, President, Koppers Company, Incorporated

W. H. Stanley, Vice President, William Wrigley Jr. Company

H. A. Stanton, Vice President, Norton Company

W. R. Starle, Assistant Secretary, W. R. Grace and Company

J. F. Stevens, Manager, Industrial Division, Metasco Incorporated

R. E. Stewart, Export Manager, Koehring Company

H. P. Stewart, Director, International Operations, Eversharp, Incorporated

R. M. Stewart, President, South American Mines Company, Incorporated

Carl A. Sundberg, Secretary, American Locomotive Company

Guillermo A. Suro, Chief, Division of Language Services, Department of State

C. O. Swanson, Treasurer, Commerce Oil Corporation

C. O. Swayzee, Chief, Division of International Labor and Social Affairs, Department of State

W. F. Tempest, Office Manager, Portland Cement Association

Alfred Teshen, President, The Inland Steel Company, Incorporated

R. H. Thornton, Editor in Charge, Ginn and Company

J. M. Tompkins, Placement Director, Vick Chemical Company

W. S. Tower, President, American Iron and Steel Institute

Gladys E. Townsend, Director of Services, Travelers Aid Society of New York

W. U. Townsend, Export Manager, National Gypsum Company

Argus Tresidder, Director of Communications, Joseph E. Seagram and Sons, Incorporated

A. B. Troeger, Assistant Office Supervisor, Export Department, General Machinery Division, Allis-Chalmers Manufacturing Company

Park B. Turner, Manager, Export Sales, Jones and Laughlin Steel Corporation

B. W. Van Riper, Educational Travel Division, American Express Company

W. A. Vela, Export Manager, Graflex, Incorporated

A. A. Verner, Sales Manager, Export Division, The Kelly-Springfield Company

W. E. Vincent, Foreign Department, Quaker Oats Company

R. Vizcarrondo, Foreign Sales Manager, The Baldwin Piano Company

T. L. Vogel, Foreign Freight Traffic Manager, Union Pacific Railroad Company

Charles B. Wade, Jr., Personnel Department, R. J. Reynolds Tobacco Company

E. H. Wagner, Employment and Personnel Division, Swift and Company

E. H. Walker, Secretary, Committee for Economic Development

B. H. Walton, Allyn and Bacon

W. A. Weber, International Division, Ford Motor Company

M. Wellerson, Director of Export, Washburn Crosby Company

Alex J. Wertis, Personnel Manager, United States Steel Export Company

Nate White, Director of Information, Committee for Economic Development

R. L. White, Treasurer, Tennessee Eastman Corporation

W. C. White, President, Alcoa Steamship Company

F. H. Wickhorst, Director of Personnel, Procurement and Training, Kaiser Services

George Wilgus, Personnel Director, The Mutual Life Insurance Company of New York

C. E. Williams, Employment Manager, Packard Motor Car Company

R. E. Williams, Chief, Overseas Affairs Division, Office Director of Civilian Personnel, Department of the Air Force

W. E. Williams, New York Personnel Manager, Union Carbide and Carbon Corporation

R. E. Wilson, Chairman of the Board, Standard Oil Company (Indiana)

H. Carl Wolf, Managing Director, American Gas Association

R. A. Wolff, Manager, International Division, Albert Trostel and Sons Company

W. G. Wood, Executive Department, General Electric Medical Products Company

R. E. Woodruff, President, Erie Railroad Company

W. E. Worcester, Vice President, Kinney Manufacturing Company

James B. Young, Vice President, Barber Steamship Lines